KEEPING UP WITH A
REVOLUTION

KEEPING UP WITH A
REVOLUTION

The Story of
United Methodist Communications
1940 - 1990

EDWIN H. MAYNARD

United Methodist Communications
Nashville

*This book is dedicated
to the two great loves in my life—
Eleanor and the family
Staff colleagues in the work of communication*

e. h. m.

ISBN 1-878946-01-3

Printed and bound in the United States of America

Contents

Preface

"Communicating the good news of God's transforming grace and reconciliation of the world through Christ is the mission of the church"—General Commission on Communication, October 1987.

If we are God's people we cannot be silent and still be faithful.

This book tells how, over the past fifty years, The United Methodist Church called forth dedicated, creative people to help it communicate that good news within the church and to the world.

The players changed from time to time, but the goal remained the same, to help the church tell its story.

From 1946 until his retirement in 1984, Dr. Edwin H. Maynard was a key player on the communication team. As an editorial director, assistant general secretary, scholar and teacher he is eminently qualified to write the history of United Methodist Communications and its predecessor agencies.

These pages will be a lasting treasure for communicators and historians alike. The past has inspiration and lessons for all of us.

United Methodist Communications has published *Keeping Up With a Revolution* to celebrate its fiftieth birthday and to celebrate the talent and dedication of hundreds of writers, producers, secretaries, reporters, librarians, camera and sound technicians, engineers, artists, accountants, telephone people and administrators who made this story happen.

The word communication shares the same Latin source as the word communicant—one who shares the Eucharist or Holy Communion. To help the church communicate the gospel is a high calling indeed.

Roger L. Burgess, General Secretary
United Methodist Communications
April 1990

Acknowledgments

*T*he author wishes to thank Dr. Roger L. Burgess, William R. Richards and the Executive Staff of United Methodist Communications for recognizing the need for a history of UMCom's first fifty years, from 1940 to 1990. It is good that this can be written while memories have not failed and documents can be found.

It has been a unique advantage that the author has a personal memory of a major part of the events covered by this history. However, it could not have been written without significant help from many sources. In particular I wish to thank Dr. Burgess and the UMCom staff for their support at every point.

My research has been aided by Rosalyn Lewis and the staff of the library of the United Methodist Publishing House in Nashville, Elmer O'Brien and the staff of the library of United Theological Seminary in Dayton, C. David Lundquist and the staff of the General Council on Ministries in Dayton, and staff of the Archives of The United Methodist Church in Madison, New Jersey, especially Mark C. Shenise.

Also to be thanked are present and former UMCom staff who have helped with research and have reviewed text, especially Arthur West, Harry C. Spencer, Howard Greenwalt, Gene Carter, Curtis A. Chambers, Nelson Price, Donald E. Collier, Peggy J. West, Thomas McAnally, Tony Pilversack, Edgar A. Gossard, Ben Logan and Robert Lear.

Staff help has been contributed by Suzanne Price, Maggie Tucker, Betty Van Dyke, and Anne Carey in research and picture search and by Dee Hinkle in production. Joretta Purdue has been most helpful as copy editor and consultant on many details of the manuscript.

Finally, I must thank my wife, Eleanor, for her constant encouragement and services as reader, consultant and sometime taskmaster.

e.h.m.

Introduction

Jesus, telling parables on the mountainside, used the communication medium of choice for his day: storytelling.

One of the first Christian converts, the Ethiopian eunuch, heard the Good News face-to-face from Philip, using the high tech of the time—a papyrus scroll. Thus the apostle antedated by nearly two thousand years today's slogan of "high tech/high touch."

During the Middle Ages stained-glass windows and murals told Bible stories to people who had no access to the book.

Martin Luther used the new technology of his time—printing from movable type—to put Scriptures into the hands of the people. And in England John Wesley took prolific advantage of the print medium.

In America, as around the world, churches have published books, newspapers, magazines, tracts and lesson materials in abundance.

It would be preposterous to suggest that the church has only recently learned to use the media of mass communication. This history of United Methodist Communications from 1940 to 1990 makes no such claim. But it is fair to say that at no time in the history of the church have those who would communicate the Good News seen radical media changes pile so rapidly one upon another. Events of these years have been called a media explosion and a communication revolution. Both are correct.

Hence the title of this book: *Keeping Up With a Revolution.*

Communicators in what is now The United Methodist Church, like their peers in all denominations, have found undreamed-of opportunities in one new media development after another. At the same time they have faced enormous costs in using the new media. The times have made a rigorous demand for setting priorities and selecting media that are both effective and affordable.

While the seeds of the communication revolution had been sown earlier, it happened that the explosion of electronic media began about the same time that Ralph Stoody was opening his little office in New York. With that office United Methodists began to build a structure to enable an intentional approach to the media. Other offices were created in response to perceived opportunities and needs, and eventually they were joined into what we now know as United Methodist Communications.

It is a story that has its share of mistakes and missed opportunities, but it is even more a story of foresight, creative innovation and faithful stewardship. It affirms the wisdom of those who in 1940 wanted "an intelligent church" and set in motion a method whereby skilled professional persons could represent the church in its encounter with the world through the media of mass communication.

It is an unfinished story. One hardly dares imagine what the media will look like an another fifty years. But we know that as the communication revolution continues, The United Methodist Church is equipped to find effective ways to tell the church's story through the media of the day.

Whatever happens between now and 2040 will build on the base established between 1940 and 1990 as a generation of United Methodists strove to keep up with a revolution.

·1·

The Revolution

You have just finished a long day analyzing sales reports at the computer terminal in your "electronic cottage." Having sent your analysis to the home office over the telephone line, you sit down for a few minutes of relaxation.

Idly you pick up the remote control for your TV set. Problem: which of the 200 channels available via your dish antenna will you watch?

You decide on the channel provided by a group of church denominations and are pleased that you have hit a time when one of the United Methodist programs is on.

Just as you are engrossed in a segment about the spiritual life of Native Americans, the phone interrupts.

It's your husband, on a business trip out of town. "Hi, Hon! How are things?"

"Busy, busy."

"Did you remember to transfer funds at the bank to cover that check for Jill?"

"Oh gosh, it slipped my mind. I'll do it right away."

"Good! And another thing. I'll be able to get home Thursday afternoon, so we can take in that play you wanted to see."

"Great! I'll get the tickets."

"Bye. See you Thursday."

Outdoors it's raining hard, and the bank is closed, but no matter. By the flip of a switch your television set becomes a banking terminal. After you've entered your code, the screen displays account information. Using a key pad you transfer the funds and sign off. Then you connect with the ticket outlet, select seats for the play and give the number of your debit card for payment. At once you hear a whirring sound from the back of your TV set as a miniature printer creates two tickets for Thursday evening.

Relax again. The phone again. Surprise! It's Jill calling to report safe arrival in Tokyo on that trip of a lifetime. Her voice seems almost clearer than Jim's when he phoned.

Quiet again. You reflect on the ease with which you do errands that used to require hours of running around. And you remember reading that phone calls from Asia are so clear because the sound is carried by a light beam through a tiny glass tube stretched under the Pacific Ocean and that 40,000 phone conversations could be carried simultaneously through that tube, each one clear and not mixed with others.

That moment of your afternoon is an incident of the future because today few homes are equipped for all of those communications. But the technology exists now, in 1990. Much of it is already being used. In a few years thousands of families will be transforming their TV corner into a communication center.

Already many individuals are running businesses from their homes, using computers and sending computerized information over telephone lines. Add a fax machine, and written messages or pictures go over the wire.

These are just a few pieces of what is called "the communication revolution."

Fifty Years Back

Think back fifty years from the year 1990. In 1940 many families—but by no means all—had telephones. The really modern ones had dial phones; others placed calls through manual operators. Long distance calls were expensive and difficult to hear.

Newspapers—more than two thousand dailies in the United States—enjoyed a near monopoly as carriers of information, although radio was growing. That year there were 862 radio stations in the United States—all of them transmitting by AM (amplitude modulation).

Television was a dream. It had been demonstrated at the Chicago World's Fair in 1934, and the first commercial broadcast was April 20, 1939; but American television in 1940 consisted of a handful of bulky black-and-white receivers for limited broadcasts from experimental stations in and around New York. Widespread home television would have to wait until after World War II.

Today, in 1990, television is in 98 percent of all homes, and most families own two or more sets. They receive programs from 1,342 stations broadcasting over the air, and more than half of all homes are wired for cable television. Thousands of homes have dish antennas to receive signals bounced off satellites high above the earth.

Radios are everywhere—even as we jog. Those 862 radio broadcasting stations have grown to 10,244—FM (frequency modulation) as well as AM.

Only the newspapers have declined—down to 1,657 dailies. Magazines tend to have smaller circulations than in the 1940s but have increased vastly in the number of titles.

The years from 1940 to the present have replaced the acoustical phonograph, playing 78 rpm records, with stereophonic sound via long-play records and tape cassettes. Now laser has brought us the compact disc. Sound quality is enhanced by digital recording. The visual counterpart of the phonograph is video, unknown in 1940 but now commonplace. It gives us rental movies, recorded programs from the home TV set, and the modern equivalent of home movies made with the family camcorder.

Motion picture theaters, a major form of entertainment in 1940, survive but are reduced in numbers and vastly changed to compete with television and home video.

In 1940, schools and churches used teaching pictures and perhaps a flannelgraph. A few progressive educators were using magic lantern slides or motion pictures shown with cumbersome

3

projectors. The filmstrip was on the verge of major development. Today video is the medium of choice for educators. And computers with instructional programs are in thousands of schools.

Scrambling to Keep Up

All of this—and much more—is part of that communication revolution. The church, during those fifty years, has been scrambling to keep up.

For nearly twenty centuries Christians have been gathering for worship and study and to encourage one another in the faith. The gathered community continues to be the heart of the church, though supplemented today with media that share the worship experience with persons who are ill, whose ability to leave home is limited, or who are in remote locations. Preaching the word, teaching in small classes and sharing one-to-one testimony are essential to the church. They are here to stay.

But today, as through the centuries, the church uses the media at its command to increase the range and extend the power of communication.

As we reach the year 1990, we find in-church use of media in such forms as books, church newspapers, magazines, newsletters, films and filmstrips, and video. To reach beyond its walls the church uses radio and television, video, the news media, advertising, public relations and public events. Computers—one of the most powerful and versatile communication tools yet invented—serve within the church and support its outreach.

Has the church kept up with the communication revolution? No, and it never will.

We have seen vast change in communications during the past fifty years, and one can scarcely imagine what the next fifty will bring. The years of rapid change have placed upon the church a heavy burden of learning about new communication tools, understanding what they do best—and cannot do—and evaluating benefits versus cost. In no way could the church make full-scale use of every new communication opportunity.

4

Yet in a sense the church *has* kept up with the communication revolution. The church has done this by wisely establishing structures for communication. Beginning in 1940, what is now The United Methodist Church has had agencies assigned to work in the media. In this way it has built a corps of communicators who understand the techniques and technologies of the media and are committed to serving the church.

These communicators—hundreds as professionals and thousands as volunteers—are people who in 1990 as in 1940 help the church tell its story.

·2·

Before the Beginning

This is the story of United Methodist Communications, a church agency that has struggled to keep abreast of the communication revolution and help the church tell its story.

United Methodist Communications—known familiarly as UMCom—celebrates its fiftieth anniversary in 1990. Its founding dates from October 1, 1940, when the Rev. Ralph W. Stoody opened his "Methodist Information" office in New York.

While the institutional history begins with 1940, one can scarcely say that The United Methodist Church and its antecedent denominations only then began to communicate. John Wesley was not only a preacher, but an author and publisher. Circuit riders in America carried books in their saddlebags. Dr. Stoody's new office built on the work of others who had gone before.

The printed page was used from the start in the Methodist family of Christians. Charles Wesley published books of hymns. John Wesley wrote 233 books and pamphlets and established *The Arminian Magazine*.

In the American church, printing and publishing have been institutionalized in the United Methodist Publishing House, and its story, dated from 1789, is told elsewhere. For 150 years books, newspapers and magazines were the church's major—almost exclusive—use of communication media other than preaching.

Newspapers of the Church

Official publications of the Methodist Episcopal Church are dated from 1826, although annual conferences had established *Zion's Herald* in Boston in 1823 and the *Wesleyan Journal* in South Carolina in 1825. Nathan Bangs responded to an appeal by several conferences for a churchwide newspaper. In September 1826 he brought out the first issue of *Christian Advocate*, which the 1828 General Conference authorized retroactively.

That paper had a long and distinguished history. It was a newspaper of general circulation, then an in-church newspaper, sometimes issued in regional editions. Later it was a weekly newsmagazine, and finally a monthly magazine for the clergy until the name was retired in 1976.

Notable in the long line of *Advocate* editors were Bangs himself; Thomas Emerson Bond, Sr., who influenced events at the separation of the church in 1844; the Rev. James Monroe Buckley, whose editorial crusade began Methodist sponsorship of health and welfare institutions; James R. Joy of the New York edition; the Rev. Claudius B. Spencer in Kansas City from 1900 to 1932; the Rev. Dan B. Brummitt in Chicago; the Rev. Roy L. Smith, who helped cement church union after 1939; and the Rev. T. Otto Nall (later bishop), who guided the *Advocate* through major changes as church publications were being modernized in the 1950s.

A *Christian Advocate* for the southern church was established after the Methodist Episcopal Church divided in 1844. It was edited by the Rev. W. P. King in 1939 when three Methodist denominations reunited. The southern *Advocate* and the several regional editions in the North were merged into a single national *Christian Advocate*—the weekly newsmagazine mentioned above.

Zion's Herald at one time merged with *Christian Advocate* and later resumed independence. It continues today, serving New England United Methodists as an edition of *The United Methodist Reporter*. Through the years numbers of annual conferences have had their own publications, many using the name *Christian Advocate* and many surviving to this day. *The United Methodist Reporter* dates from 1847 as a conference paper in Texas, making it one of the country's oldest publications. Now national with scores of editions, it is unofficial at the national level, but it provides editions that are official publications of a number of annual conferences.

Other venerable publications were the *Religious Telescope*, begun in 1834 by the Church of the United Brethren in Christ, and *The Evangelical Messenger*, started by the Evangelical Association in German in 1836 and in English in 1848. Upon formation of the Evangelical United Brethren Church in 1946 the two merged as a weekly paper, *The Telescope-Messenger*. In 1962 it was replaced by a semimonthly family magazine, *Church and Home*, which was merged with the Methodist *Together* after the Evangelical United Brethren Church and The Methodist Church united in 1968.

United Brethren, Evangelicals and Methodists all had publications in the German language at various times. *Die Christliche Botschafter*, then 110 years old, was the oldest Protestant periodical in German in the United States when discontinued at the end of 1946. The Methodist Episcopal Church had *Der Christliche Apologete*, published in Cincinnati.

Church boards also published magazines from time to time, some quite influential. A long-standing voice of missions has been *World Outlook*, now *New World Outlook*. A devotional guide, *The Upper Room*, has achieved one of the largest circulations of any religious publication.

Maud Turpin's Press Bureau

The Methodist Episcopal Church, South, prior to the reunion of 1939, had its small-circulation, churchwide *Christian Advocate*, but church news was published largely in weekly papers of annual conferences. In that media mix a woman with pioneering instincts, Maud M. Turpin, recognized that thousands of persons—inside as well as outside the church—depended upon the public press for information about the church.

Descended from a line of fervent Methodists, including one who took part in the Christmas Conference of 1784, Maud Mooney Turpin began her career in 1914 as a writer for the Women's Missionary Council, a part of the Methodist Episcopal Church,

South, based in Nashville, Tennessee. (In the practice of the time, she was of course always *Mrs.* Turpin—and in some references "Mrs. C. W. Turpin" rather than Maud.) In 1918 she joined the publicity department of the Methodist Centenary Movement, a campaign to celebrate 100 years of Methodist missions.

From that vantage she saw the need for a systematic approach to daily and weekly newspapers. She persuaded church officials to put her into that business. With a meager budget, contributed in small sums from general boards of the denomination, she began the Secular Press Bureau in 1922. The bureau was her private enterprise, serving the boards and paid for by them, but not an official agent of the church.

Turpin coined the slogan, "Religion Is News," printed it on her letterhead, and sold the idea to newspaper editors across the South. She sold her idea to church officials with a survey of editors who said they would print more news of the church if it were provided in professional form. Then she challenged the editors to make good on their promise.

Maud Turpin got to know editors personally all across the South and was welcome in many a news room where supposedly gruff city editors would offer the use of a typewriter for her own work. In one year she counted 100,000 column inches of Methodist news in 400 papers. Each summer she transferred her operation to Lake Junaluska, North Carolina, the "summer capital of Southern Methodism," a practice she continued until 1949.

She was also a pioneer as a woman news writer at a time when newspaper staffs were largely male. She was sometimes called "the dean of southern newspaper women" and at her death in 1959 was eulogized by newspapers she had served. For a time she was president of the Tennessee Pen Women's Association.

With the establishment of Methodist Information by the new Methodist Church, Stoody asked Turpin to continue her work from her Nashville base, and on January 1, 1941, she became "southern manager" of Methodist Information, a title she held until her retirement in 1947.

Turpin was noted not only for her pioneering spirit, but for her professional skill and long hours of work. Once asked about the bureau's office hours, she replied: "We don't observe hours; we just do our work."

The Publicists

In the North the Methodist Episcopal Church had no direct counterpart to Turpin and her Secular Press Bureau, but communicators were at work, often calling themselves "publicists." One was Irish-born William Watkins Reid, whose byline became familiar to thousands as W. W. Reid from the time he joined the staff of the Board of Foreign Missions in 1919 until his retirement in 1961. He traveled widely to gather information and write stories publicizing missions. He wrote a syndicated column, "On a Wide Circuit," from 1946 until retiring.

Reid's avocation was hymnody, on which he became an authority. For years he was an active member of the Hymn Society of America, and a number of his hymns were published by the society. He was author of four books. From 1940 until 1956 he edited *The Pastor's Journal*, a publication of the Board of Missions of The Methodist Church.

Reid in 1929 was one of the founding members of the Religious Publicity Council (now Religious Public Relations Council). He was also active in the Methodist Press Association, an informal fellowship of the editors of church-related papers and magazines, much later to broaden its perspective as the United Methodist Association of Communicators. He often hosted MPA meetings, since the favorite gathering time was meetings of the Board of Missions. Editors were eager to cover the board, and Reid, among other duties, was its press officer.

In the audiovisual area the Rev. Hiram G. Conger, working for the Methodist Episcopal Church from a Chicago base beginning in the early 1920s, collected a file described as hundreds of thousands of negatives and photographs, particularly on missions. He also created slide lectures, using big glass lantern slides, sometimes hand tinted. "Hi," as he was known, was transferred to the Board of Missions in New York after the 1939 union.

Reinhold Rickarby, another pioneer in audiovisuals, worked in Chicago with Hi Conger as darkroom technician. Rickarby came to New York with Conger in 1940 and continued at the Board of Missions.

During World War II the board hired a Japanese-American, Toge Fujihira, in the shipping department. It was discovered that he had photographic skill, and he became the board's principal photographer, continuing until his death in 1973.

A pioneer Methodist broadcaster was the Rev. Walter Van Kirk, who was on the staff of the Federal Council of Churches. He was on national radio each week with commentary on religion.

The 1928 Methodist Episcopal General Conference consolidated publicity and promotion previously done by each church board for its own interests. Publicity for agencies supported by the central benevolence fund, World Service, became the responsibility of Miron A. Morrill. Previously a teacher and public relations director of Hamline University, he came to Chicago in 1929 to take up the work. He prepared posters and leaflets and worked with newspapers and radio. He edited a church bulletin service, printed on one side with general information, leaving the back for local imprinting. He started a short-lived magazine, *World Service News*, a victim of the Great Depression.

The 1932 General Conference returned promotion to the agencies. Dr. Morrill then became publicity director for the Board of Education, still in Chicago, and he continued until 1940. The 1936 General Conference reestablished centralized promotion, and the board loaned Morrill's services to the Council of Secretaries for a promotional effort called Million Unit Fellowship Movement.

To get radio time, Morrill retained Homer Buckley, a Catholic layman in the firm of Buckley, Dement and Co. Buckley recruited Lou Cowan, who had created national prominence for band leaders Kay Kyser and Wayne King—and who was Jewish. (Cowan later was to become president of the Columbia Broadcasting System's television network.) This tri-faith trio created a series of radio dramas, *Heralds of Destiny*, offered to radio stations as phonograph records. By the end of the first season some two hundred stations were using them. One of the participants was an operetta star, singer Jeanette MacDonald, a Methodist.

It was Cowan, the Jewish publicist, who suggested a national observance in 1938 of John Wesley's Aldersgate experience, after learning from Morrill the story of Wesley's conversion. They took the idea to Ernest Lynn Waldorf, bishop of Chicago and head of the

Commission on World Service and Finance. The outcome was a three-day "Council on the Future of Faith and Service," attended by more than 4,000 persons. Cowan and Morrill received an unexpected assist when Bob Feller, star pitcher for the Cleveland Indians and a Methodist, dropped by. The church convention was pictured on sport pages across the country.

Morrill was asked to direct press relations for the Uniting Conference of three branches of Methodism in Kansas City in April and May 1939. He was assisted by Burr Hupp. The Rev. Walter Van Kirk handled radio coverage. Commentator on a preconference radio broadcast was Alfred M. Landon, 1936 presidential candidate and titular head of the Republican Party. News releases and texts of documents were provided to local reporters and wire services.

After the Uniting Conference Morrill teamed with the Rev. J. Manning Potts of Virginia and the Rev. Elmer T. Clark of Tennessee to arrange exchange visits between North and South by bishops of the new denomination. At the 1940 General Conference Morrill was again in charge of press relations. Shortly thereafter he returned to college teaching, though he was secretary of the Commission on Public Relations and Methodist Information until 1957.

Later reflecting on his career, Morrill wrote: "I was a propagandist. Is there such a thing as good legitimate propaganda? If not, what has the preaching of the Gospel been for two thousand years?"

Methodist Protestant Publications

The Methodist Protestant Church, third party to the union of 1939, made no structured approach to the public press, but in-church publications carried information to members. The Board of Missions and the Board of Christian Education co-operated in training persons to carry the missionary message into local churches. The missions magazine was *Missionary Record*.

Prior to 1929 the denomination had two general publications, *The Methodist Protestant*, published in Baltimore, and *The Methodist*

Protestant Recorder, from Pittsburgh. *The Methodist Protestant* claimed to be the oldest weekly in American Methodism, tracing an unbroken line from *Wesleyan Repository*, established April 12, 1821, in the Philadelphia Conference by William S. Stockton, a layman and one of the Methodist Protestant founders. After three years it gave way to *Mutual Rights*, edited 1824-28 by the Rev. Samuel K. Jennings. Among its editors was the Rev. Nicholas Smethen, a founder of the denomination and noted preacher and educator.

The *Recorder* dated from 1839 when, under auspices of the Pittsburgh and Ohio Conferences, the Rev. Cornelius Springer began publishing the *Western Recorder* near Zanesville, Ohio. Although the Methodist Protestant split from the Methodist Episcopal Church was on issues of freedom and democratic church government, the denomination had its own struggles with freedom of the press. At its 1838 General Conference a resolution was proposed to exclude any content about slavery from the official organ, the *Methodist Recorder*. The Rev. George Brown, later to become editor, killed the proposal by pointing out that the Methodist Protestant Constitution provided "no rule shall be passed infringing the liberty of speech or of the press." However, when the Rev. Thomas Stockton, newly elected editor, arrived in Baltimore to start work, he learned that the Baltimore Book Committee was imposing a similar restriction. He resigned.

Another noted editor of the *Methodist Recorder* was the Rev. Lyman Edwyn Davis, for several terms president of the denomination and one of its historians.

Declining circulation and financial pressures led to merger of the two publications in 1929 as *The Methodist Protestant-Recorder*. The decline continued, however, and the public media were seen as competition rather than opportunity. In its report to the 1932 General Conference the Board of Publication complained: "The radio, automobile and movies have made such inroads on the time of people that they have little time left for religious reading. These modern inventions account for many of the present day ills of our people."

Other Publicists

Other persons working in various aspects of communications prior to 1939 were the Rev. Richard T. Baker in the Methodist Episcopal Board of Foreign Missions (later dean of the journalism school at Columbia University); the Rev. Elmer T. Clark in the Board of Missions of the Methodist Episcopal Church, South; the Rev. Charles A. Britton, Jr., of the Georgia Methodist newspaper, later with the Methodist Publishing House; Jay S. Stowell and Sarah Evans (later as Sarah Evans Kinney, editor of *The Methodist Woman*) of the Methodist Episcopal Board of Home Missions; the Rev. Boyd McKeown in the Division of Educational Institutions; and Methodist Protestants the Rev. R. L. Shipley, editor of the *Recorder*, and the Rev. C. S. Johnson in Sunday school literature.

All of these—and many others—laid the foundations on which the lasting communication structures of the church were built, beginning in 1940. They were the pioneers, before the beginning.

·3·

An Intelligent Church

Bishops of the church in 1939 asked for "an intelligent church." To achieve that, they asked for "a department of Methodist intelligence."

It sounds quaint today. We would say "an informed church." But whatever the language, the intent was clear.

That was the year of Methodist reunion. Healing breaches that had occurred in 1828 and 1844, the Methodist Episcopal Church; Methodist Episcopal Church, South; and Methodist Protestant Church came together to form The Methodist Church. The Uniting Conference was held in Kansas City, Missouri, in May 1939. Bishops of the three uniting denominations had prepared an Episcopal Address to point directions for the new church.

In their address the bishops observed that "Methodism in this great day finds itself with large numbers of communicants and adherents who have little knowledge of its activities, plans, purposes, happenings and movements. They are not, except in the most meager way, Methodistically informed." They pointed to the "great publishing houses" (three, not yet united), but asked for use of "the greatest modern agencies for taking the message of this church to its own people and all people."

The recommendation was referred to the conference's Committee on Education, which interpreted the idea as "a Department of Promotion and Publicity which is to be supported by the boards and

15

other agencies," adding that "perhaps the agents already at work in the field of publicity and promotion in the several boards may be co-ordinated to discharge this responsibility."

The committee then recommended, and the Uniting Conference agreed, that the bishops should appoint a committee to study the matter and report to the General Conference the following year.

The committee consisted of Bishop G. Bromley Oxnam; Bishop Ivan Lee Holt; the Rev. Roy L. Smith, pastor of First Methodist Church, Los Angeles, and soon to become editor of *The Christian Advocate*; and William F. Bigelow, longtime editor of *Good Housekeeping* magazine.

"Methodist Information" Is Established

The committee's report, rather than pooling the publicity efforts of the various boards, called for a new and independent agency to "gather news of public interest concerning Methodist activities and opinion and disseminate it through the secular press, the religious press, the radio, and other legitimate media of public information." It was to be known as the Commission on Public Information.

Dr. Smith, reporting in 1940 for the committee, reminded the conference that some persons had argued for a Methodist daily newspaper after the model of the *Christian Science Monitor*. Then he noted that "we already have in the United States at least twelve hundred daily newspapers which are open to the news of The Methodist Church. Somebody else is paying the bill . . . and their columns are open to us for our news. The proposal would . . . get this type of information into the newspapers, through the radio and other public means of information at the minimum possible expense." (His figure was low. There actually were 2,015 daily newspapers in the United States in 1940.)

There was no debate—only a few parliamentary maneuvers that failed—and the conference adopted the report. Methodist Information was born—with an annual budget of $25,000.

In a sense, the work of the new agency had already begun. A press room was provided at the Uniting Conference and the first regular General Conference. For 1940 the General Conference Committee on Publicity and Press Relations consisted of the Rev. Elmer T. Clark, formerly of the southern church; the Rev. Crates S. Johnson, formerly of the Methodist Protestant Church; and the Rev. Miron A. Morrill, formerly of the Methodist Episcopal Church. Some seventy reporters received press credentials in 1940, including one Ralph Stoody, who represented the *Christian Science Monitor*.

The first Commission on Public Information was well acquainted with the media. It consisted of Bishop Oxnam and Smith from the study committee; William A. Bailey, editor of the Kansas City *Kansan*; Josephus Daniels, editor and publisher of the Raleigh *News and Observer*; the Rev. Umphrey Lee, president of Southern Methodist University; and B. E. Chappelow, a St. Louis advertising man. Bishop Oxnam was chairman. Chosen as treasurer was the Rev. Walter W. Van Kirk, already engaged in radio work with the Federal Council of Churches.

Enter Ralph Stoody

At the organizing meeting in July, the commission chose as director the Rev. Ralph W. Stoody and designated New York as headquarters.

Dr. Stoody was to be prominent in communication circles of the church for 24 years, until his retirement in 1964. A courtly person with distinguished, if premature, white hair, he was often likened to a Kewpie doll. Always the gentleman, he was polite and considerate in his dealings. He loved his staff and was solicitous of their families, and the staff reciprocated. Yet he could be tough in dealing with a news crisis.

Born in Rochester, New York, Stoody was educated at Ohio Wesleyan University and Boston University School of Theology. Between college and seminary he was an editorial associate for *Epworth Herald*, a youth publication. He served churches in Vermont and Maine. In 1934 he became pastor of Union Church in Fall River, Massachusetts, and while there earned (in 1939) a doctorate at the Gordon School of Theology and Missions in Boston. His dissertation was a monumental study of the development of religious journalism in the United States. In 1959 he wrote *A Handbook of Church Public Relations*, for years the definitive work in its field.

While at Fall River in the 1930s he also studied at Harvard and Columbia Universities. For a number of years he had been writing for newspapers and magazines, including the *Christian Science Monitor*.

Stoody's office opened October 1, 1940, at 150 Fifth Avenue, in a building occupied by the Methodist Publishing House and the Board of Missions. In November, the day after the presidential election, he purchased office furniture at half price from the New York campaign office of the loser, Wendell Willkie.

Stoody began creating files of information, photographs and personal data about prominent Methodists. He made contact with his counterparts in other denominations to study their methods, and he got to know persons in the newspaper, broadcasting, publishing and advertising fields.

One day as he lunched with an advertising man, his partner asked about his annual budget. When Stoody said $25,000, the man protested, "No, no, I didn't mean your salary, I meant your budget." Truly the church expected much from what looked like very little on Madison Avenue.

Stoody had a reputation for good luck, especially in catching trains at the last minute and getting hotel rooms without reservations. But the staff teased him about his unlucky choice of automobile: He purchased an Edsel, the Ford Motor Company's greatest fiasco. An amateur magician and ventriloquist, Stoody delighted in entertaining children by making coins and candy appear in strange places.

Staff and Offices Are Added

One of Stoody's early decisions was the deployment of staff. General agencies of the new church were scattered among seven cities, but it was determined their news interests could be served by offices in the three locations of greatest concentration: New York, Chicago and Nashville. For Nashville, Stoody called upon Maud Turpin, whose press bureau there became the southern office of the new agency. For Chicago he engaged George B. Ahn, Jr., a University of Michigan journalism graduate with editorial and publicity experience in Detroit. Ahn was also a "local preacher" (licensed to preach but not ordained).

The two new offices opened officially January 1, 1941, and soon the name Methodist Information—or MI—was being used for everyday operations. During the remainder of the quadrennium the fledgling bureau focused on news coverage via newspapers and radio. However, some work was done in promotional campaigns and in public relations training.

In its report to the 1944 General Conference the commission could point to an impressive record of news dissemination: getting feature stories in newspapers and magazines and placing personalities on radio. Co-operating with the new denomination's $25,000,000 campaign for postwar relief and reconstruction, the Crusade for Christ, Methodist Information arranged for a segment to appear on the newsreels popular in theaters of the time. *News of the Day* estimated that sixty-five million people saw the Crusade for Christ in newsreels.

In radio Methodist preachers were being placed in regular rotation on Sunday programs of the Columbia and Mutual networks. Through the Federal Council of Churches two Methodist personalities appeared regularly on NBC and the Blue Network. They were the Rev. Ralph W. Sockman, whose program, *National Radio Pulpit*, was to run for many years, and Dr. Van Kirk, who did a program on *Religion in the News*. The director himself was given air time on more than one occasion.

Methodist Information placed with 200 independent radio stations a 13-program series of fifteen minutes each on the Crusade for a New World Order. MI produced, and the Methodist Publishing House paid for, a series of Roy L. Smith's radio meditations on the Twenty-Third Psalm.

Stoody served on the Joint Radio Commission (later Protestant Radio Commission), related to the Federal Council of Churches.

A New Approach

Without question the church's new communication agency rested on the work of those who had gone before. But it was unique in its mandate to represent the entire church and to relate to public media. Most of the immediate predecessors of Methodist Information saw themselves as publicists, by definition trying to bring support to a particular agency or program.

True, during the early years of the nineteenth century some of the church publications had been general newspapers, reaching a broad public with news of the day. That is how the *Christian Advocate* in the 1820-30s could be described as having the largest circulation of any newspaper in America (25,000 in 1828). But that stage ended rather quickly, and the periodicals came to be addressed to in-church audiences.

Even the bishops at the 1939 Uniting Conference seemed to be thinking in-church when they called for "an intelligent church." But those who drafted the legislation set the course with a larger vision. The 1940 *Discipline* provided that the Commission on Public Information should "gather news of public interest concerning Methodist activities and opinion and disseminate it through the secular press, the religious press, the radio, and other legitimate media of public information."

When the commission was formed, it included among its six members two prominent newspaper editors. The tradition thus established was followed through the years as William A. Bailey and Josephus Daniels were succeeded by such Methodist newsmen as Milburn P. Akers, editor of the Chicago *Sun-Times*; Grove Patterson, editor of the Toledo *Blade*; Holt McPherson, editor of newspapers at Shelby and High Point, North Carolina; Alvah Chapman, general manager of the Miami *Herald*; Louis Spilman of the Waynesboro *News-Virginian*; Pat Patterson, founding editor of *Black Enterprise*; Walter Magronigle, senior vice president of a prominent fund-raising firm; and two journalism school deans: Burton Marvin of the University of Kansas and Quintus C. Wilson of the University of West Virginia, later of Northern Illinois University. Their presence on the commission helped to establish

Methodist Information perspectives and set its standards. From the start MI saw itself as representing the church to the news media and its news values as those established by professional journalists.

Through generations of church publications, most of the editors had been clergymen first and editors through on-the-job training. Methodist Information hired clergy for its staff only if they had prior experience with newspapers. Through succeeding years the vast majority were laity whose skills came from journalism schools and work experience.

While MI sometimes assumed the role of publicist, as when Stoody got the Crusade for Christ into newsreels, the main task was seen from the start as purveying the news of the church factually and objectively while not hesitating to report bad news with the good. This practice quickly established a high level of credibility with newspaper reporters and the wire services.

Credibility also came from Stoody's philosophy of church communications. He expressed it on the last page of his book: "Backing up the broadcast and the news story, the form letters and the parish paper, the signboard and the poster, the glowing spire and the landscaped edifice, there must be reality. There must be a church that is the church. There must be a fellowship of Christians worshiping together, studying together, working together, building better lives, a better community, and a better world."

It was a busy start-up time. In 1944 Methodist Information entered its second quadrennium as a fully operational public relations agency for the church.

·4·

The Church in the News

*T*hey were tumultuous times. The 1940s were wartime and postwar; the '50s had McCarthyism, blacklists and witch hunts; the '60s saw protest and confrontation. These were the years during which Methodist Information began its work and grew as a voice of the church to the public.

The primary task was seen as press relations—providing news releases, answering questions, and operating news rooms at major events. Efforts focused on general newspapers and church publications, though attention also was given to radio until the Radio and Film Commission became functional in 1952.

Led by the Rev. Ralph W. Stoody, supported by other staff and members of the commission, the philosophy was to be an objective and reliable source of news. Staff were enjoined not to mingle promotion and news and to release only stories a city editor would deem newsworthy. They were cautioned never to withhold news simply because it might seem negative. At the same time they were to see themselves as representatives of the church and the Christian message.

Along with the news function, Methodist Information quickly saw a need to offer training in public relations and to develop a corps of public relations specialists. During the years of its independent existence—from its formation in 1940 until it became a part of United Methodist Communications in 1972—Methodist

Information (later United Methodist Information) pursued this goal. There was a crescendo of activity directed toward educating and then placing the persons trained on public relations committees and sometimes in professional posts in episcopal areas and annual conferences.

To reflect its operating name, the commission name was changed in 1952 from "Commission on Public Information" to "Commission on Public Relations and Methodist Information." And insiders liked to refer to the entire operation as "MI."

A Time of Expansion

After four years the budget inched up from $25,000 to $26,500, and continued operation depended in part on free rent from the Methodist Publishing House in Chicago and Nashville. By the end of the second quadrennium the Council of Bishops urged a budget increase to $100,000. That was not to be, but MI did receive an annual budget of $75,000 from 1948 to 1952. Then it went up to $110,000 and in 1956 to $140,000.

Encouraging as these increases were, the money seemed never to be quite enough. A crisis erupted when the 1968 General Conference voted to freeze the budget at the level of the previous quadrennium ($163,400) and drastic curtailment was avoided only with an emergency grant by the Council on World Service and Finance of an additional $26,600 a year.

As finances permitted, there was a progressive expansion of offices to enhance MI's services. Because persons in the Western Jurisdiction felt isolated in the days before air travel was common and because many newsmakers were among missionaries coming and going through West Coast ports, MI opened a part-time San Francisco office in 1946. This arrangement continued until several area public relations offices had been established in the West by 1952. The San Francisco office was staffed by Carolyn Wintjen, an experienced journalist who also represented the Board of Missions.

A fourth full-time national office was opened in Washington, D.C., in 1956 to cover news of church agencies headquartered there and of frequent church events in the nation's capital. In 1968 an office was opened in Dayton, Ohio, because union of the Evangelical United Brethren and Methodist Churches placed some national church offices there.

The Rev. Daniel L. Ridout joined Methodist Information in 1944 as a part-time "representative to the Negro press." The then-segregated Methodist Church had a Central Jurisdiction composed of Black churches. Ridout's job was to feed into Methodist Information the news from those churches and to offer African-American newspapers stories deemed of interest.

Ridout was a district superintendent in the Delaware Conference of the Central Jurisdiction (later assistant to the bishop). Like W. W. Reid, he could communicate through the arts as well as the typewriter. For years he directed the Baltimore Great Hymns Choir, which he founded, and he was a consultant to the committee that prepared the 1964 hymnal. Uninhibited by ethnic differences, he delighted in signing letters to white friends as "your beautiful blue-eyed brother."

A few years later three other part-time correspondents were added to Ridout's network so there could be a Black representative in each of the four episcopal areas that made up the Central Jurisdiction. This arrangement continued until the segregated jurisdiction was abolished at the time of the 1968 church union.

Other Changes

The southern veteran, Maud Turpin, retired in 1947 and was succeeded in the Nashville office by Sam Burgess, recently graduated from the journalism school of the University of Georgia. In 1950 he was succeeded by O. B. Fanning.

Fanning, known to friends as "OB," had trained in journalism at the University of Alabama. He started his career as a reporter and city editor for the Huntsville *Daily Register*. From there he moved into public relations with the Goodyear Tire and Rubber Company and the Nashville branch of the American Red Cross.

Fanning worked the Nashville beat for six years and, like Turpin before him, spent summers handling news out of Lake Junaluska.

24

One of his favorite reminiscences from Nashville years was how he got a photograph of the legendary Harry Denman, lay evangelist and for years head of the Board of Evangelism. Believing that having his picture published was unacceptable vanity, Dr. Denman refused to have a photo made. Fanning teamed up with Bob Bell, religion writer for the Nashville *Banner* and during a meeting OB engaged Denman in conversation while Bell slipped up with a camera, called "Harry" and snapped. It turned out to be an excellent picture and was distributed widely to the press—with no complaint from Denman.

In 1956 Fanning opened the Washington office, continuing there until 1960, when he went into college and conference public relations work in Florida.

West Joins the Staff

At Chicago George B. Ahn, Jr., served for some four years and was succeeded by Mary James (later Duner). Upon her resignation in 1948 it was decided to add an associate director at Chicago. Tapped for that spot was the Rev. Arthur West, a Missourian serving a church in Maine, where he was also religion editor for the Bangor *Daily News*.

As a high school youth he worked for a small-town paper. During his college years at Missouri Wesleyan and Baker University he did some newspaper writing. After studying for the ministry at Boston University he became a pastor in New England. Before moving to Maine he had been a pastor at Warren, Rhode Island, and then for two years full-time religion editor of the Providence *Journal* and *Evening Bulletin*. He had worked with Dr. Stoody in press relations for the World Methodist Conference in Springfield, Massachusetts, in 1947 and the General Conference at Boston in 1948.

Dr. West served in Chicago for sixteen years, and when Stoody retired in 1964, West was the unanimous choice of the commission to become director. He moved to New York to take up the director's duties and was replaced in the Chicago office (by then located in Evanston, Illinois) by Robert L. (Bob) Lear, a native West

Virginian who came to MI by way of journalism school in Missouri, newspaper work in Oklahoma, and area church public relations in Iowa.

West guided the agency through years of expansion, particularly development of the network of conference and area public relations specialists. He was also involved in the runup to the 1968 union and the restructure that led to formation of United Methodist Communications in 1972.

A staunch defender of open meetings and press access to information, he won his spurs in a celebrated encounter with the indomitable Dutchman, W. A. Visser 't Hooft, general secretary of the World Council of Churches (WCC). West was on loan as photo director in the press room of the WCC Assembly in Evanston, Illinois, in 1954 and proposed to make photographs of the six persons who had been nominated for the council's presidium. Visser 't Hooft objected because, by his sense of propriety, no photo should be made until the election was completed. West stood his ground and prevailed.

Staff Transitions

With Fanning's transfer to Washington, the Nashville post was taken by William M. (Bill) Hearn, a graduate of the University of Missouri School of Journalism who had done public relations for Union College in Kentucky, reported for the Louisville *Courier-Journal*, and worked at public relations for the Louisville Area of the church. He continued in Nashville until 1968, when he resigned to pursue other public relations interests.

Hearn was succeeded in Nashville by Thomas S. (Tom) McAnally, an Oklahoman who held a master's degree in journalism from Syracuse University and had been a reporter in Oklahoma prior to becoming director of public relations for the Nebraska Annual Conference. He was later to become director of United Methodist News Service within United Methodist Communications.

In 1960 Winston H. Taylor became the second person to staff the Washington office. After study at Willamette and a degree from

Tulane University, Taylor had been a reporter for the *Statesman* in Salem, Oregon. Then for seven years he directed Methodist area public relations in San Francisco. While there he had written a helpful booklet, *Angels Don't Need Public Relations*. He directed the Washington office until 1982, earning a master's degree in communication at the University of Maryland along the way.

A veteran church journalist, Leonard M. Perryman, joined the Methodist Information team in 1967. Once a reporter for the Kansas City *Star*, Perryman had come to New York as assistant to W. W. Reid at the Board of Missions. Upon Reid's retirement he had succeeded him as director of the board's Department of News Service. Under an agreement negotiated by West, he continued part time as information director for the board, devoting the remainder of his time to the New York office of MI—about to become United Methodist Information. This freed West to take the headquarters to Dayton and personally serve the news needs there. Eventually Perryman became full-time with the communication agency, working in news and also with *The Interpreter* magazine until his death in 1983.

For twenty-nine years, 1950-79, anchor person in the New York office was Charlotte O'Neal. As administrative assistant she was aide to Stoody and West, managed the office, and co-ordinated a staff that had scattered bases and were often on the road.

The office location in New York remained at 150 Fifth Avenue until 1959, when the Interchurch Center opened. Church offices of many denominations and MI joined other Methodist agencies in moving to the 475 Riverside Drive address. The office remained there except for a few years at the Church Center for the United Nations in the 1960s.

Press Relations

With news dissemination the number one job, annual reports often began with enumeration of the releases sent out. For example, for 1969 the record read: 672 news stories, eighty-six photos, and fifty-six features and special stories sent out. The staff attended 110 out-of-town meetings and forty-three others in their own towns.

Of all the Methodist meetings, General Conference required the most effort and it was the General Conference news room in which staff took the most pride. Prized mementoes were letters from reporters from the Associated Press or major newspapers complimenting the news room performance.

The 1944 conference, staffed by the still-fledgling team of Stoody, Turpin and Ahn, hosted reporters from far away despite wartime travel restrictions. In 1952, with radio relations still being handled by Methodist Information, Walter Van Kirk made three transcriptions of General Conference news. Delegates were told of more than 500 stations where the folks back home could hear his reports.

By 1956 the Radio and Film Commission was in operation and had taken responsibility for radio news coverage of General Conference. More than 150 radio and television programs on the conference were produced, and distribution included the Voice of America. For print media, some seventy-five reporters and editors were accredited to the press room.

Each quadrennial year the MI staff made the circuit of six (later five) jurisdictional conferences. At these regional meetings they reported the election and assignment of bishops, then circulated pictures and biographies of the new leaders.

Along with sending out releases and staffing news rooms, the MI team also suggested story ideas to major magazines. From this kind of initiative, and responding to inquiries when a magazine came up with its own idea, came significant articles about the church in popular publications such as *Life*, *Look*, *Christian Herald*, and *Time*. In the early '40s a *Life* picture story of a Methodist preacher used space valued at $65,000. *Life* treated the Methodists again in 1947 with a 14-page picture essay, and MI distributed 10,000 reprints. In 1964, coinciding with the General Conference, *Time* ran a color photo of Bishop Gerald H. Kennedy on the cover and carried three full pages about The Methodist Church and issues facing the General Conference.

Another vehicle for getting the word out is *Methodists Make News*, a weekly summary of major news items begun by West in 1954 and continuing to the present. First directed to the editors of local church newsletters and a few newspaper writers, it was popular enough that staff had to struggle to restrict distribution to its intended audience. It began with around 300 users and by 1970 had grown to 1,350. (Later it was restricted to church and secular journalists so that in 1990 its circulation was 675.) Established later as a parallel to *Methodists Make News* was a monthly summary, *United Methodist Highlights*, which in 1990 is sent by air to more than a hundred editors in other countries.

Training for PR

Education in public relations, another major function, was approached through seminars, publications and eventually a film. Seminars were offered to episcopal areas and annual conferences, with leadership coming from the MI staff and local news professionals. Over the years almost every part of the church had this training for interested clergy and lay volunteers.

The premier printed resource was Ralph Stoody's book, *A Handbook of Church Public Relations*, published in 1959 by Abingdon Press. Also circulated were booklets: *Improving Your Church's Public Relations* by Arthur West (50,000 printed), *Churchmen, Let's Go to Press* by commission member Holt McPherson, and *Public Relations in the Local Church* by O. B. Fanning.

The motion picture was titled *As Others See Us*, and 100 16mm prints were circulated, plus 200 in the newly developed super-8 system. The film was used also by two Canadian denominations.

For many years the headquarters office maintained a lending library of books on journalism and public relations, sent free on request to anyone interested.

With Methodist Information for a name, the office attracted hundreds of inquiries beyond the routine questions from newsmen. The staff perpetuate many legends about some of the offbeat questions. Perhaps the prize query came from a Midwestern college planning to give an honorary degree to President William S. Tubman of Liberia, who happened to be a Methodist. The college wanted to know Tubman's measurements so a proper size academic gown and cap could be provided.

The Oxnam Hearing

The period from the union of 1939 to the union of 1968 brought many adjustments in American life. The church was caught up in much of the turmoil, and public relations staff faced agonizing choices.

Responding to a postwar fear of Communism, two congressional committees captured headlines. In the Senate it was a committee dominated by Sen. Joseph McCarthy of Wisconsin. In the House of Representatives it was the Committee on Un-American Activities, chaired by Rep. Harold H. Velde of Illinois, who happened to be a member of a Methodist church. The committee had assembled files on thousands of citizens—many of these files containing press clippings and miscellaneous printed pieces filled with rumors and undocumented accusations of Communist sympathies.

One such file pertained to Bishop G. Bromley Oxnam of the Washington Area, one-time head of the Methodist Commission on Chaplains and a forceful spokesperson for human rights. The committee staff had begun sending out copies of contents of its Oxnam file on letterhead, giving the impression of official endorsement of slanderous allegations. The situation reached a crisis when Rep. Donald L. Jackson, a member of the committee, publicly declared that the bishop "served God on Sunday and the Communist front for the balance of the week."

Bishop Oxnam demanded a hearing before the committee. Charles C. Parlin, noted New York attorney and for many years a member of the Commission on Public Relations and Methodist Information, advised him. Stoody was his public relations consultant. On July 21, 1953, the bishop had his hearing. Neither Parlin nor Stoody was permitted to speak, but Oxnam ably pled his own case. He refuted the charges against him and chastised the committee for its practices. Sometime after midnight the hearing adjourned with his vindication.

Press coverage of the event was enormous. Immediately Methodist Information and the Commission on Promotion and Cultivation joined to distribute across the church a 12-page tabloid telling the story, largely by means of press reports and comment by noted columnists and commentators of the day: Walter Lippman,

Marquis Childs, Doris Fleeson, Dorothy Thompson and Eric Sevareid.

There were other witch hunts in those times. Stanley High wrote an article on "Methodism's Pink Fringe," published in the *Reader's Digest* in 1950, attacking leadership of the Methodist Federation for Social Action, but the *Digest* refused to publish a reply. In 1960 there was controversy over a U.S. Air Force manual that contained slurs against some church organizations.

Social protest dominated the next decade. The 1964 General Conference had protesters holding a prayer vigil demanding abolition of the Central Jurisdiction. The 1970 special General Conference was surrounded by demonstrators pressing Black demands.

A "Black Manifesto" was issued in 1969 by James Forman, demanding of white society reparations for past injustices. Many persons could not be convinced that Methodist money was not somehow funding the movement. There were sit-ins at the Board of Missions offices.

Such issues, along with a crescendo of protest against the war in Vietnam, called for constant attention by the news staff.

At Lake Junaluska, Fanning had to deal with conflict over racial segregation of the swimming pool. When Black students protested their exclusion from the pool, Fanning put out the story over objections from the chairman of the board of trustees. It was years later that, after a communion service, the chairman sought out Fanning and said "all is forgiven." Fanning recalls, "At first I didn't know what he was forgiving me for, but then it dawned on me that he had held the pool integration story against me for a long, long time."

Area PR Programs

The establishment of area offices of public relations began in 1949 when the Rev. Wesley E. (Wes) Brashares, who had been experimenting with public relations in Wisconsin, was invited by Bishop Richard C. Raines, new chairman of MI's commission, to come to Indiana to direct an area-wide pilot program.

Brashares survived with aplomb when the printer returned his first batch of news release headings imprinted "Office of *Pubic* Relations" and went on to create a program that was widely imitated. Added in 1950 were area offices in Ohio, Texas, Georgia and Kentucky. Early conference offices were set up in the Chicago Area by Rock River and Illinois Conferences.

In 1950 the budget contained $10,000 for subsidy to area programs. The offer was that if an episcopal area would establish an office of public relations, staffed with a qualified person and co-operating with the national office, $2,000 would be granted the first year, $1,500 the second, and $1,000 the third. Thereafter local funding was expected.

Area after area accepted the offer and for years Methodist Information annual reports contained the latest tally. After twenty years MI could point to a network of thirty-eight affiliated area and conference offices. The final grant was $500 to the New Jersey Area in 1970. By then thirty-one areas had been given financial aid totaling nearly $200,000.

The area offices, like the national MI, were expected to give primary attention to press relations. For significant events in their area they were to be news reporters for the national organization. Frequently they would add local angles to national stories for placement in newspapers of the area. They were also expected to offer training in public relations. In many areas the PR director also edited a small newspaper or an area news supplement for *Christian Advocate* or, later, *Together*. Increasingly the area offices got into radio and television.

Building a Network

As public relations staff persons came to be deployed in area offices across the church, Methodist Information built them into a network with frequent consultations, a newsletter and periodic "all-staff conferences." The first was held on St. Simon's Island, Georgia, in 1953, the second in New York in 1954, and the third at Bloomington, Illinois, the following year. They continued for a long time at near-yearly intervals, featuring professional improvement and idea exchange through speakers and panels—plus the opportunity for the public relations practitioners to get to know one another.

The St. Simon's Island gathering was memorable not just for the training it provided. Carolyn Williams, director of the Atlanta Area PR office, had prevailed upon a high-school music director to have a brass band at the railway station in Brunswick for arrival of the overnight sleeping car from Atlanta that carried most of the participants. The Pullman car also carried a newly elected state legislator coming home from his first session. His grateful grin faded fast as he realized it was not his constituents who had brought the band and that the "keys" to the city of Brunswick and the Golden Isles were for Ralph Stoody and Arthur West.

Upon his retirement, Stoody was honored by creation of a fellowship for graduate study by a young person interested in church-related communications (Chapter 14). The first fellowship of $1,000 was awarded for the school year 1965-66. Soon the award was raised to $2,000 a year and then $3,000. In 1981 the fellowship was renamed "Stoody-West," extending the honor to Arthur West, and the award was $5,000. Later it was raised to $6,000.

As church union approached in the years leading up to 1968, MI people were in frequent contact with their Evangelical United Brethren opposite numbers. The EUB General Conference of 1962 created a Department of Communication related to the Council of Administration, with the Rev. Paul V. Church as executive and the Rev. Curtis A. Chambers as secretary. Those two joined forces with Methodist communicators to handle press relations for the 1966 simultaneous General Conferences in Chicago and the Uniting Conference in Dallas in 1968.

Prior to 1968 there was much talk about the structure for communication—whether it should be unified or scattered through the church organization. Decision was deferred while a study commission worked, and what had been MI remained separate as United Methodist Information in the first quadrennium after union. While prizing independent status as an impartial news bureau, the staff supported the holistic approach. The 1972 General Conference joined United Methodist Information with other units in what became United Methodist Communications.

33

·5·

Joining the Revolution

*T*he communication revolution that today expands in quantum leaps began quietly in the nineteenth century. Photography began in the 1840s. The telegraph came in 1845, followed by the telephone, 1876; phonograph, 1877; and wireless telegraphy, precursor of radio, 1896.

Print, which long had reigned alone as *the* medium of mass communication, was not standing still. The linotype machine, faster presses, automatic feeders and folders, and finally the rotary press made printing faster and cheaper than ever. Offset printing, later to dominate the field, was being developed.

But it was in the audio and visual fields that changes were most dramatic. The photograph, first a novelty, then a family keepsake, became a major element in newspapers and magazines, reproduced by halftone cuts from the 1880s on. About the same time came the glass slide that could project an image onto a screen, then motion pictures, and by the 1930s "talking pictures."

Meanwhile radio was becoming a major medium of communication, having developed from the first American commercial broadcast in 1920 to 1,500 stations on the air by 1948. Television, demonstrated at world's fairs in Chicago in 1934 and New York in 1939, had perhaps 250,000 sets in use by 1948. In short years the TV set would be in nearly every home and revolutionize the way we get our news, our relaxation and our values.

34

Predecessors of today's United Methodist Church did not call it a communication revolution, but they recognized the power of newly developing media. In the early years of the twentieth century, staff of church boards began to use photographs to tell their story. The "magic lantern" excited churchgoers with slides that told about missions.

Hi Conger's move to New York with his collection of photos and lantern slides (Chapter 2) speeded the use of pictures in The Methodist Church's Board of Missions. By 1945 the board established a Department of Visual Education. The same year there was an Audio-Visual Department in the Division of the Local Church of the Board of Education. Other boards, with smaller budgets and staffs, often made audio and visual education a part of someone's portfolio. In 1944 three boards and the Methodist Publishing House assigned their audiovisual staff to co-operate in producing a motion picture for the Crusade for Christ.

The church was awakening to the incipient revolution.

Spencer and Tower

Major figures in development of The Methodist Church's electronic communications were the Rev. Harry C. Spencer and the Rev. Howard E. Tower, who first got into audiovisual work in the Mission and Education boards, respectively.

Spencer was born in Chicago, son of a minister who soon moved the family to Oregon. His parents, both amateur photographers, gave him a Brownie box camera for his tenth birthday. While working as a janitor at the local library during his high school days, Harry was drawn to a back corner where photography magazines were shelved and spent his spare time there.

In 1925, with a degree from Willamette University but no job, he took his mother's advice and enrolled in a business school in Portland. He learned typing and shorthand—skills that soon got him a position in the legal office of the Union Pacific Railroad in Portland.

Though attracted to a career in law, young Spencer felt a call to the ministry. So he returned to the Chicago area to study at Garrett Biblical Institute (now Garrett-Evangelical Theological Seminary). He followed a Garrett degree with a master's in English literature at Harvard. In 1931 he was ordained and began his ministry in Chicago.

While in his second Chicago pastorate, he came to the attention of the Rev. Ralph E. Diffendorfer, executive secretary of the Division of Foreign Missions in the Board of Missions. After using him as secretary for a hearing in Chicago, Dr. Diffendorfer recommended Spencer to the board for the staff position of recording secretary. In 1935 he went to New York to take the job.

While he did secretarial work, Spencer's interest in photography became known, and he was asked to take occasional pictures or give photographic advice. In 1941 he toured the Caribbean with a 35mm camera and the new color film. His 35mm slide set on Cuba was a first for the board. Then he was asked to edit a missionary's movie film on Japan. In 1945 when the board's various audiovisual interests were consolidated, Spencer was put in charge.

Indiana-born Tower was educated at DePauw University and Boston University School of Theology and stayed in New England after finishing his theology degree. He held student pastorates while studying at both schools and in 1931 was ordained elder. For six years, 1937-43, he was executive secretary of the Board of Education of New England Southern Annual Conference. After a two-year pastorate at Bridgewater, Massachusetts, Tower's skills in Christian education attracted the attention of the General Board of Education in Nashville, where the Rev. Nathaniel Forsythe had a portfolio that included religious education in mass communication. Within that area, Tower was placed in charge of audiovisuals.

Before long Tower and Spencer became aware of their parallel jobs. They first met at Lake Geneva, Wisconsin, where the International Council for Religious Education was holding a training conference on audiovisuals. They began to share ideas about how the agencies and individuals interested in audiovisuals might co-ordinate their efforts to the benefit of all.

36

A Beginning in 1948

Others had the same thought, particularly those in an audiovisual task force of the Council of Secretaries. By time of the 1948 General Conference, some of the bishops had the idea too. Ten annual conferences and the Council of Secretaries had petitioned for an agency to be formed.

Interest in use of the new media was offset by financial restraint. The result of committee work and General Conference debate was an awkward compromise. The conference did indeed establish a commission, but there was no money and no staff. Most members of the commission were to represent the church's various boards. The budget was to be whatever the boards were willing to contribute. Staff would be co-opted from the boards. In the *Discipline* it was called "Interagency Commission on Audiovisual Materials" but it soon took the name "Radio and Film Commission."

The commission's mandate was "to unify and co-ordinate the audiovisual programs of all Methodist agencies dealing with projected pictures, recordings, transcriptions, radio and television programs, and other audiovisual materials."

Tower was elected "chairman of the joint staff" and Spencer secretary. Both continued on the payrolls of their respective boards and carried their previous responsibilities. The "joint staff " consisted of audiovisual staff persons of the other agencies: Elizabeth (Betty) Marchant, Woman's Division of the Board of Missions; Howard Ellis, Board of Evangelism; Walter N. Vernon, Jr., Editorial Division of the Board of Education; H. S. Van Deren, Jr., Methodist Publishing House; Earle H. MacLeod, promotional office of the Council of Secretaries; and the Rev. Ralph W. Stoody of Methodist Information.

Bishop Donald H. Tippett was elected chairman, a post he was to hold for sixteen years. Tippett's interest was sought because he had been pastor of First Church, Los Angeles, and was acquainted with the Hollywood scene. First recording secretary was Walter Vernon, also to serve until 1964.

Considering the rivalries among the boards and their jealousy for every penny of the World Service Fund that supported them, expectations were not high. The occasional meetings of the joint staff did little joint planning; rather, each person announced to the others what his or her agency intended to produce.

The Wesley Film

The setup as voted by General Conference stressed co-ordination and seemed to presume that work of the church in radio and film was the sum of agency productions. The legislation contained little to see whole the work of electronic communications, nor to recognize that the local churches and the denomination had needs beyond the collective interests of the boards.

And yet from the awkward arrangement sprang one of the most popular and durable projects in the communication history of United Methodists: the John Wesley film.

J. Arthur Rank, an English Methodist, was the premier film producer in his country and owner of major production facilities. One of his staff, Noel Evans, came annually to North America, and Tower and Spencer became acquainted with him. Their conversations led to the idea of a film on Methodism's founder, inspired in part by the recent Lutheran success of a film on Martin Luther. A Wesley film would find audiences on both sides of the Atlantic. Rank and his organization would be the major English contribution. The Americans, even with no budget, pledged financial backing. Tower organized a committee under aegis of the Radio and Film Commission, and a production contract was signed with Rank's Religious Films, Ltd. The Rank firm later handled distribution in Great Britain.

Bishop Charles C. Selecman, recently retired, agreed to look for the money needed. By an ingenious plan, any church that paid $100 to the project was promised one of several hundred "premieres," which meant the first showing in its vicinity. Bishop Selecman was able to enlist 524 churches toward a production cost of $154,000, and he found donors of other funds. Floyd Woodcock, a Delaware layman, also raised money for the film.

By the 1952 General Conference the Radio and Film Commission (by then calling itself RFC), was able to announce a release date in 1953 and generate churchwide excitement for the film. It was filmed in England by the Rank organization from a script written in both countries. It employed an experimental color negative film not yet in commercial use. The Eastman Company sold RFC the first 50,000 feet of the film.

After 524 local premieres, the movie was shown in 3,470 churches during its first sixteen months. First showings were for whatever an offering brought; later there was a rental fee.

Through the years *John Wesley* was released not only as the 77-minute feature film, but as a 15-minute short version (*Wesley and His Times*) in the original 16mm format and in Super-8. Both eventually were redone as videos. The 15-minute film was released in Spanish in 1970. The long and short versions in both formats continue in use. They were widely shown in 1988 as the church celebrated the 250th anniversary of Wesley's Aldersgate experience.

A Viable Commission

The Wesley film and extensive radio and TV coverage of the 1952 General Conference in San Francisco helped delegates see the potential of the new media. Walter Van Kirk's commentary was heard over 480 radio stations, and conference personalities were placed on TV in San Francisco and Los Angeles. Tapes and records were offered to delegates, and before leaving they witnessed a motion picture of conference highlights. The Radio and Film Commission was continued, now made functional with staff and a slice of the World Service pie: a little under 2 percent, or up to $175,000 a year.

It happened that in 1952 the church was in the midst of one of its periodic restructures. In authorizing an independent, funded Radio and Film Commission the General Conference rejected a study commission's proposal to put all communication work into one agency—a holistic approach whose time had not come.

In the newly empowered commission, Bishop Tippett was continued as chair, and Dr. Tower and Dr. Spencer were asked to leave their board positions to work full-time with the commission. Spencer became executive secretary and Tower associate. Work began in the summer of 1952. The first offices were three basement rooms in Nashville provided rent-free by the Board of Education. But the question of a permanent location raised issues that were to haunt the agency for years: What is its mission? What priority is assigned to serving denominational agencies? Should production facilities be owned by the RFC or rented as needed? How important is it to have easy access to professional directors, actors and technical personnel?

New York, Chicago, Los Angeles and Nashville were considered. Spencer favored New York for access to broadcasting executives, filmmaking talent and peers in other churches. But the decision of the commission (still composed largely of board representatives) was for Nashville—a strong tilt toward the role of serving audiovisual needs of church agencies.

As the organization began to take shape, more staff were needed. One of the first hired was Anton J. (Tony) Pilversack, who had gone from his native Minnesota to New York, where he had a commercial art studio across the street from Harry Spencer's office in the Board of Missions. They formed a friendship, and Pilversack worked on some of Spencer's productions at the board. He was invited to join the staff in Nashville. There he played major roles in production, equipment design and maintenance, and building design until his retirement in 1983, and indeed for a number of years beyond as part-time consultant.

It was Pilversack whom Spencer, in the early days, asked, "How does a radio work?"

The answer was, "Why don't you build one and find out?" So Spencer bought the parts and soldered them together under Pilversack's guidance. The results were a radio that lasted twenty-five years and learnings that would last a lifetime.

Joe W. Davis was brought in as treasurer and business manager and the Rev. John Clayton as supervisor of production.

Radio and Television

Radio placement of Methodists on national programs, begun by Methodist Information, was picked up by the RFC in 1952. The commission worked with the Upper Room (Board of Evangelism)

40

as consultant to its radio ministries. Training was offered to persons interested in local broadcasting.

Television was growing rapidly as measured by the number of stations and sets in homes. During 1952-56 two programs were offered to TV stations. First was *The Pastor*, a 15-minute weekly program. The first 13-week series was placed on 144 stations and a second on 115.

More ambitious was *The Way*, thirteen half-hour dramas, one of which recounted how commission chairman Tippett had lost an eye in an assault which resulted in a turnaround in the life of his assailant. Most of the filming was done in Hollywood.

In the quadrennium RFC produced or supervised sixty-four motion pictures and fifty-six filmstrips.

The agency went to the 1956 General Conference with a request to add "television" to its name. In fact, television had been a part of the assignment in the *Discipline* from the start, but it had been deemed not politic to include it in the name.

What had been RFC emerged from General Conference as Television, Radio and Film Commission, before long taking the easily pronounced acronym TRAFCO. The budget was enlarged, and the agency focused its attention on developing children's television.

Staff Development

To do the work a larger staff was built, but not without pain. Within that growing staff, three names are forever linked:

The Rev. William A. Meadows began working in radio while a pastor in Michigan. He came to TRAFCO as director of radio and television services and training.

The Rev. W. Carlisle Walton, Jr., who had spent several years in industry before preparing for the pastorate, was added to the TRAFCO staff to develop the children's television ministry.

The Rev. Royer H. Woodburn had been a pastor and Wesley Foundation director before coming to TRAFCO from Minnesota. His assignment was to assist churches in the use of audiovisuals.

On February 3, 1959, the three attended a meeting in Chicago planning a radio program sponsored by the Board of Lay Activities. That evening they flew to New York to be ready for a TV Ministry meeting the next day. They were excited about riding in a new aircraft, the turbo-prop Electra. As the plane approached LaGuardia Field in New York, it plunged into the East River, and most of the passengers were lost, including Meadows, Walton and Woodburn.

It was a devastating blow to TRAFCO and a loss of life in duty with few parallels in the history of church agencies. Memorial services for the three were held in the Upper Room Chapel; memorial chapel furniture was installed in the TRAFCO building; and a Children's Television Endowment Fund was established in their memory.

As staff was rebuilt, one who came was Nelson Price, an Iowa layman who had been part of the Methodist Information network as director of public relations in Chicago and Indiana. Another was the Rev. James C. Campbell of Mississippi and South Carolina, who began as director of utilization. Both would later become associate general secretaries of UMCom.

Others who served during the TRAFCO years and not mentioned previously include Duane M. Muir, Robert C. Glazier, Lyman White, the Rev. Gene W. Carter, the Rev. Sam S. Barefield, Edgar A. Gossard, Ben T. Logan, J. Fred Rowles, Donald E. Hughes, Sue Couch, C. B. Anderson, Bruce C. Mosher, William R. Richards, Charles Washburn, Jeff Whatley, Herschel Pollard and Vilmars Zile. Rowles and Gossard were producers and Hughes a director, all winning numerous awards. Logan was a producer and highly regarded script writer and in private life author of several books. Dr. Carter specialized in relationships with annual conferences.

Iowa-born Carter attended Simpson College, Garrett Theological Seminary and Northwestern University. He returned to Simpson 1946-52 to teach sociology and direct the Warren County Group Ministry, widely heralded as a model for rural churches. He went to California to teach at Pacific School of Religion and was a district superintendent in California-Nevada Conference 1960-61, coming to TRAFCO in 1961.

42

William F. Fore, later to head the Broadcasting and Film Commission in the National Council of Churches and to become a distinguished critic of the media, served briefly as a consultant.

The Use of Radio

Placement of Methodist speakers on network radio programs was done mostly through the interdenominational Broadcasting and Film Commission (BFC), which became a part of the National Council of Churches in 1950. Syndicated programming in the Methodist name came particularly through the Methodist Series of *The Protestant Hour*, sponsored by a consortium of denominations and based in Atlanta. That program continues to the present.

Popular for many years was NBC's *National Radio Pulpit* featuring the Rev. Ralph W. Sockman, pastor of Christ Church in New York, under arrangements made with NBC by the Broadcasting and Film Commission.

As network radio gave way to network television and radio went local, new emphasis was given to helping annual conferences and local churches work in radio. Part of that was accomplished by providing training, but there was a useful service: *The Word—And Music.* Offered to pastors who wished to broadcast, it provided weekly scripts, resources for developing one's own script, and recorded music. It was begun in 1964, and at its peak there were 250 local broadcasters. When changing patterns lessened demand, it was discontinued in 1988, after twenty-four years and 1,250 program scripts.

Night Call

Most creative of the radio programs was *Night Call*, which contributed to national dialog in 1965-66 and again in 1968-69. It was the first national phone-in show and required electronic equipment not yet in existence. TRAFCO commissioned Warren Braun, a consulting engineer, to do research and development.

Specifications were formidable. The telephone signal must go out over the radio clear and intelligible; it must be possible to block out objectionable language; the caller must be able to hear both ends of the conversation; and more. Braun came up with solutions and later improvements; sixteen patents were held by TRAFCO.

The technology was adopted by other radio call-in shows, although today a small silicon chip can do what two hundred pounds of *Night Call* equipment did at the time.

Night Call went on the air in April 1966 as a late-night national forum on critical issues of the day, and it ran for eleven months. Although it built up to a network of twenty-five stations and others were interested in joining, it was terminated for financial and technical difficulties. Listeners phoned questions on public issues and ethical concerns to guests, who were also on long distance lines. Among those presented by host Russ Gibb were Frank Laubach, the literacy pioneer; Charles Schulz, cartoonist; and Rodney Shaw, staff of the Board of Christian Social Concerns.

Nineteen sixty-eight was the year of the assassination of the Rev. Martin Luther King, Jr.; riots surrounding the Democratic National Convention in Chicago; and ghetto protests, non-violent and violent. The TRAFCO staff looked for ways to be a reconciling influence and decided to reactivate *Night Call* as what *Time* Magazine dubbed "the cool hot line." Its goal was to maintain dialog between Whites and Blacks in hope that communication might calm the atmosphere. Logan was producer, and Richards was network announcer. Host Del Shields aired such national figures as Black author James Baldwin, civil rights advocate Ralph Abernathy, boxer Muhammad Ali, politician Sargent Shriver, and playwright Arthur Miller. The Black activist Stokely Carmichael drew a record 64,440 calls. At its peak it was being carried by 117 radio stations. Since many were clear channel stations, the signal pretty well blanketed the country. Many of the staff were Black.

The revival of *Night Call* had been scheduled for the fall of 1968, but as the "long hot summer of '68" began, the broadcast date was moved up to June 3. With a yearly budget of $450,000 of largely non-existent funds, the program limped along on emergency grants, winning more praise than money. It reaped awards and was lauded by the New York *Times, Christian Science Monitor, Newsweek* and *Saturday Review*. Following a brief try at commercial sponsorship, it was terminated in September 1969, after a 16-month run.

Among other radio shows were *Man With the Mike*, begun in 1965, and *American Profile*, which succeeded it in 1967. Both featured interviews with ordinary persons who were making contributions to their communities. The latter tested commercial sponsorship with limited success, although at one time it was carried by more than five hundred stations. *The Place* offered music and conversation for teenagers.

More Use of Television

In television *Talk Back* was an innovative half-hour show with fifteen minutes of filmed drama posing a moral or ethical dilemma, leaving fifteen minutes for a local panel to discuss the issue. A filmed discussion was available as fallback, but local teams were urged to bring community persons to the station for their own discussion. More than 5,000 local panelists appeared in two 13-week series.

Talk Back was first offered to TV stations in October 1958, and distribution was under auspices of the Broadcasting and Film Commission of the National Council of Churches. One station program director called it "probably the best approach to religious programming I have seen" because it dealt with everyday topics and had local follow-up.

Breakthru was the first children's program. It was made available to conferences and churches for placement on local TV channels. In fifteen months its thirteen segments were on 128 stations. As it began in 1961-62, sixteen regional workshops were conducted to train local church persons in placement and use of *Breakthru*.

For *Breakthru* and *Talk Back* some fairly well-known Hollywood personalities came to the TRAFCO studios, including Martin Balsam and a young Patty Duke. Some episodes were filmed in Hollywood. John Clayton was a frequent director.

Because television is such an expensive medium, funding was always a problem. The general budget from World Service, which by 1967 had risen to $340,000, could not cover television costs. There was never money to purchase air time; such money as was available was used for production, relying on local Methodists for placement. And it was found that despite clamor to "see my church on the tube," the TV Ministry did not have popular appeal for fund-raising outside World Service.

Back in 1953 emergency authority had been given for a TV Ministry Fund of up to $296,000 a year. The 1956 General Conference authorized solicitation of special gifts of $1,000,000 a year, but the most received was a quarter of that. The TV Ministry Fund was continued in subsequent quadrenniums, and in its last years prior to the 1968 union the fund usually brought in around $300,000 a year. The problem of funding the church's television ministries would continue far into the future.

Along with producing programs, TRAFCO encouraged men and women to look at television critically. An ambitious Television Valuation Project in 1967 asked church members to monitor programs during October, discuss them and report to local stations and TRAFCO. More than 2.5 million viewer's guides were used.

Film Production and Distribution

Meanwhile the Nashville studios were busy turning out hundreds of productions for church agencies. Filmstrips were the bread-and-butter products, but there were many motion pictures. Among them were some produced for the Commission on Promotion and Cultivation, a future partner in UMCom.

It was a time of growing popularity of audiovisuals for teaching and other program use in the churches. TRAFCO worked with the Board of Education to train church people to use AV materials effectively. In the four years from 1956 through 1959, for example, the studios turned out fifteen motion pictures and nineteen sound filmstrips for in-church use in addition to productions for radio and television. Among the films were *One Love—Conflicting Faiths* for the Board of Education, *The Stepsitters* for the Methodist Youth

Fund, and *A Better World Begins With Me* for the Board of Evangelism.

Most production was for clients, but on rare occasions TRAFCO was able to create a film useful to local churches but not tied to the interests of any board. Notable was *The Coming of the Stranger*, a Christmas allegory scripted by Logan and produced in 1967. It was popular for many years. There were occasional forays into theatrical short subjects, such as *Hello Up There* and *Gold Is the Way I Feel*.

Busy as the studios were with TRAFCO's productions, there was occasional "down time." To minimize losses, a tax-paying, wholly owned company was formed to rent out facilities and equipment—often with production personnel. It was called Kingswood Productions and through the years it helped offset the costs of studio operation.

Distribution was not a major function for TRAFCO. Clients took delivery on films produced for them and arranged their own distribution, frequently through the Methodist Publishing House.

The Persistent Question

Location was a question that had come up back at the agency's beginning and would not go away.

Not long after the Radio and Film Commission in 1952 set up shop in borrowed quarters, it rented an abandoned church as a makeshift studio. Then in 1954 came a chance to rent space in a building that had been erected for RCA. In its studios a young Elvis Presley had made some of his first recordings. For a time RFC, and after 1956 TRAFCO, used part of the building, then leased it all, and in 1959 bought it. It was 1525 McGavock Street, Nashville, the agency address for twenty-six years.

The early years at 1525 McGavock were the glory years of studio production for films, before the shift to documentaries and location shooting. Producer Don Hughes recalled later how filming was done all day, then a night shift would tear down the sets and build new ones for the next day's filming. It was a busy and crowded place, later overflowing into neighboring buildings.

The rental and purchase were accomplished only with constant struggle. Where should the agency have its headquarters and what should its mission be? Yet each decision that was made increased technical capacity and committed TRAFCO more deeply to production for the church agencies.

The location question came to a boil again in 1962 when a study by a management consultant, H. Wilkes Wright, revealed that general boards of the church thought TRAFCO's prime obligation was to them, and they were not satisfied with production services being rendered. At the same time local churches and conferences had communication needs that were not being met. Wright urged reorientation from being mainly a producer of audiovisuals to "an organization of communication experts."

Relocation to New York was considered. At a meeting in February 1963 commission members were sharply divided but after long debate kept the headquarters in Nashville and established two branch offices—as Dr. Wright had recommended.

A New York office was to relate to national media, direct research and provide services to annual conferences. Carter was put in charge of the New York office.

Howard Tower and Lyman White were dispatched to California to establish a Hollywood office. Its purposes were to influence commercial film and TV producers with higher values and moral standards and to provide a base for film productions using commercial facilities. In 1964 Dr. Tower resigned, critical of TRAFCO's style in approaching the entertainment industry. He returned to conference education leadership in New England, and White continued in the Hollywood office until it was closed in 1969.

The New York office was more successful than Hollywood in carrying out its assignment and in 1966 the Radio-TV Department (Price, Logan, and Mosher) was transferred there.

Broadening the Scope

But the nagging questions never went away. Production for television was curtailed, and energy was invested in broader communication concerns. Education was one of them.

Starting in 1956 annual conferences could organize their own units parallel to TRAFCO. The general TRAFCO offered training to members of conference TRAFCOs, and in some cases to local churches. During these years Methodist Information's training program centered on public relations and news gathering. The TRAFCO events focused on radio, television and communication theory. Increasingly TRAFCO assumed a responsibility for training Methodists in communication as a whole (Chapter 14).

Subsequent to the Wright study, Spencer led the staff and commission members in examining the theological basis of the church's use of the media. He was supported in this by Carter and Price. William Fore, the one-time consultant who wrote a doctoral dissertation on the TRAFCO years, credited theological understandings developed 1963-68 with shifting the agency toward a holistic view of communication.

In 1969 Spencer declared: "TRAFCO's purpose is to enable the church to become more effective at all levels in its use of media tools and more aware of the nature of communication. . . . TRAFCO is in the business of communication."

Interest in the holistic concept of communications existed in various quarters, yet history and political factors kept the church's communication agencies within their narrow specialties. As the 1968 union of the Evangelical United Brethren and Methodist Churches approached, the Joint Commission on Church Union debated structure. While major questions were referred to a four-year Structure Study Commission, the Uniting Conference created a Program Council, modeled on the EUB Council of Administration, which had a Department of Communication. After union TRAFCO found itself a division of the Program Council—its acronym intact as Division of Television Radio and Film Communication.

Joining it in that status was what had been the Commission on Promotion and Cultivation, now Division of Interpretation.

Spencer continued to head TRAFCO, his title becoming associate general secretary of the Program Council. In some respects it was a comfortable relationship. An advantage to TRAFCO was that the Program Council was a major power center of the new denomination, giving the work a stronger base. On the other hand amenability to the Program Council limited the division's power of decision making. Largely absent from TRAFCO's governing board were agency representatives (with a vested interest in the output) and electronic media specialists (whom TRAFCO in the past had sought for their expertise).

The years 1968-72 saw renewed debate of the old question of mission. The Structure Study Commission took the holistic approach and recommended consolidating communications into one agency. Although it rejected the commission's model, the General Conference of 1972 did put three communication units—including TRAFCO—together into a Joint Committee on Communications, soon known as United Methodist Communications.

Spencer continued briefly in the new structure as an associate general secretary. He retired in 1973, able to look back on forty years of the church's increasing awareness of the need and opportunity to be involved in the electronic media.

The church had joined the revolution.

·6·

When They Hear

W hen people hear the story, they will respond."
This oft-repeated affirmation by the Rev. E. Harold Mohn
summed up the motive and method of promotion over a 20-year
period. Tell the story of denominational ministries through all the
media available; depend upon the Christian spirit of church
members for a response in enabling dollars.

Those ministries depended on giving to general benevolence
funds—the World Service Fund at the heart, plus other funds,
Advance Special gifts and freewill offerings. The benevolences
supported missions, education, evangelism and other work carried
out by church agencies. Some of the funds depended on voluntary
giving—for example the offering for One Great Hour of Sharing.
Others were apportioned, meaning that each of the annual
conferences and, through them, each church was asked to give a
specified amount, calculated by a "fair-share" formula.

Promotion was a formidable task. The benevolence funds Dr.
Mohn's office began promoting in 1952 amounted to some $30
million a year. By 1972 in The United Methodist Church thirteen
promoted funds had goals that exceeded $60 million a year.
Through those years the constant effort was to tell the story of the
church at work, using posters, leaflets, films, magazines and other
media.

The Commission on Promotion and Cultivation was established

by The Methodist Church in 1952, and with church union in 1968 it became the Division of Interpretation in the Program Council. In 1972 it was made part of United Methodist Communications.

But promotion was not invented in 1952. Ancestors of the Evangelical United Brethren and Methodist Churches had always found ways to spread the word about denominational programs and benevolent causes. The much-debated question was how it should be done.

Through the years the denominations that ultimately formed The United Methodist Church established boards to carry out vital functions such as missions and Christian education. Patterns of centralized finance evolved, but much of the funding depended upon special offerings and direct gifts. Church agencies had an obvious interest in promoting those gifts. Church members were impatient with what they saw as competition among the boards, and this led to establishment of the World Service Fund in The Methodist Church and Christian Service Fund for EUBs.

If funding were to be centralized, why not the promotion? It was a touchy point of church politics.

Offices for Promotion

In the Methodist Episcopal Church a central office to promote giving for World Service was established in 1928 and directed by Miron A. Morrill (Chapter 2). But insistence by boards on their right to do their own promotion led to its abolition by the 1932 General Conference—only to be reestablished in 1936.

After the union of 1939 the Council of Secretaries, made up of the chief executives of the various boards and commissions, maintained a service department in Chicago for mailings to churches. The council arranged for publication and distribution of "Fourth Sunday Leaflets," issued each month for use in thousands of churches where a Sunday school offering for World Service was received on the fourth Sunday of each month. The leaflets had been started in the mission board but were broadened to represent all World Service interests.

The 1944 Methodist General Conference anticipated the end of World War II by setting up a four-year Crusade for Christ. Its centerpiece was a fund of $25 million for postwar relief and reconstruction. Oversight was given to a committee headed by Bishop J. Ralph Magee. Staff director was the Rev. J. Manning Potts, who had been a pastor and district superintendent in Virginia. To his Chicago office Dr. Potts brought Earle H. MacLeod, a layman with photographic skills and ad agency experience.

The Crusade was a resounding success. The financial goal was exceeded, with more than $27 million given. Its Year of Evangelism was credited with adding 1,063,000 members—578,-000 of them by profession of faith. There were glowing reports also from the Year of Stewardship, Year of Church School Enrollment and Attendance, and the Crusade for a New World Order.

On conclusion of the Crusade for Christ, Potts became editor of *The Upper Room*, a position he held for many years, and MacLeod became director of the reestablished promotional office of the Council of Secretaries. He was responsible mainly for the Fourth Sunday Leaflets.

The 1948 General Conference called for another quadrennial program, this one named the Advance for Christ and His Church. There were preaching and teaching emphases on Our Faith, Our Church, Our Ministry and Our Mission. The financial component was a system of direct gifts for specific missionary projects, a style of mission support that had been popular in the southern church but was not widely practiced in the North. Now it was to be regularized in the united church as Advance Specials. The plan also included a Week of Dedication during Lent, with a special offering for emergency mission needs and continuation of the Crusade Scholarships begun the previous quadrennium.

Bishop William C. Martin chaired the committee, which chose Dr. Mohn as executive director. A member of North-East Ohio Conference, Mohn had been a district superintendent and pastor, most recently at Warren, Ohio.

Fluent in German, Mohn enjoyed telling folks the name of his birthplace: Gnadenhutten, Ohio. He was educated at Ohio

Wesleyan and Boston Universities, receiving a theology degree from the latter in 1913. Advanced study at the University of Jena, Germany, was interrupted by the outbreak of World War I. His pastoral ministry had been marked by support for benevolences, and he gave himself wholeheartedly to promotion of Advance Specials. He brought to the staff the Rev. Oscar L. Simpson of the Holston Conference, a writer, editor and photographer.

Commission Is Established

The final report of the Advance for Christ and His Church was made to the 1952 General Conference in San Francisco, a conference that had before it a massive restructure proposal. One part of the plan would have put together in one large agency the work of promotion; television, radio and films; press and public relations; devotional and educational literature; and the publishing house. It was a holistic concept, but delegates found it too large and complex. Other agencies were left independent and the conference voted to establish a Commission on Promotion and Cultivation.

In a sense the commission was a successor to the Advance and the promotional office of the Council of Secretaries. Bishop Martin was chairman, and the staff consisted of Mohn, Simpson and MacLeod. Headquarters were in Chicago, adjacent to the Council on World Service and Finance.

MacLeod stayed on the staff until 1955 with responsibilities including stewardship cultivation and materials for churches to use in every-member canvasses. The Board of Lay Activities had an interest in stewardship, and there was a question as to where that responsibility properly belonged. The question was resolved with transfer of MacLeod and his responsibilities to the Board of Lay Activities. Eventually he became director of public relations for *The Upper Room* at the Board of Evangelism in Nashville.

With Mohn's insistence on telling the story, the staff used the communication media. Stories were told of the work of all the agencies supported by the World Service Fund—which meant almost every aspect of the church's program. Articles and pictures were syndicated to the church press. World Service leaflets were continued with an emphasis on human interest stories and pictures. Films and filmstrips were made.

One other device was used to tell the story—and it was called *The Story*. It was a quarterly publication in newsletter format on slick paper with good reproduction of photos and stories about the work supported by general benevolences. It was started in 1953, and Dr. Simpson was editor.

When the 1956 General Conference came, the commission could report impressive gains in giving for benevolences: World Service had increased from $8,136,000 to $9,761,000; Advance Specials grew in popularity with $23,549,000 given for world missions, national missions and overseas relief during the quadrennium. The commission also promoted two special offerings (Week of Dedication and World Communion), the Interdenominational Co-operation Fund, the Methodist Television Ministry and an emergency Bishops' Appeal for Korea.

But one other part of the commission's assignment had not been a success. Like most General Conferences, that of 1952 had voiced a concern for co-ordination within the church's bureaucracy. The mandate of 1952 had been for the commission to review "the several and combined plans of the general boards and agencies for the production and distribution of all free literature and promotional and resource periodicals . . . for the purpose of co-ordinating the content, distribution and timing." In addition, the commission was asked to study a 1952 proposal for combining agency publications into a monthly program journal.

The Program Journal

Many delegates to the 1956 conference expected a report that general agency publications had been combined. But Mohn protested he could not "be a policeman" at the same time he depended on agency co-operation for the promotional work. Moreover, the chief executives of those agencies sat as ex-officio members of his commission.

So the 1956 General Conference found that no publications had been consolidated and in fact a new one, *The Story*, had been started. After much corridor discussion, hot debate on the floor, and impassioned pleas for preservation of this or that publication, the conference directed the Commission on Promotion and Cultivation to "publish a free local-church program journal . . . [to present] the program and promotional materials of the general agencies in a correlated manner."

The action was seen by agencies—correctly—as a blow to their autonomy and a step toward closer co-ordination of the internal communications of the church. The editor of *The Voice* of the Board of Temperance wrote an editorial entitled "Methodist Laryngitis" and suspended publication immediately, not waiting for the new program journal. The editor was a young man named Roger L. Burgess who, after a career in other general agencies of the church, in 1984 became general secretary of United Methodist Communications.

Other publications suspended were *The Pastor's Journal*, *Shepherds*, *Church and Campus*, and *The Story*. Mohn immediately selected *The Methodist Story* as the name for the journal and by fall had selected Edwin H. Maynard, from the staff of *The Christian Advocate* and *Together*, as editor.

To represent the insights and concerns of the church agencies, an Editorial Council was formed. One of Maynard's first tasks in October of 1956 was to preside over a meeting of the council—with editors of the five discontinued publications among those around the table.

The first managing editor was Darrell R. Shamblin, later to become editor. In 1958 a Spanish edition was started. (More about *The Methodist Story*, *Spotlight* (EUB), and *The Interpreter* is told in Chapter 13).

Convocations Tell the Story

The Methodist Story began with the issue for March 1957 and was introduced at a District Superintendents' Convocation.

The DS Convocation was a prominent device in the promotional strategy of the commission. The 570 superintendents collectively covered the entire country, each responsible for a territory, supervising from fifty to more than one hundred churches, and reporting to a bishop. As Bishop Martin said to the gathering, "I could not call out the name of any town in the United States but that one of you men [and they *were* all men] could stand and say, 'That's in my district.' "

The chain of command was seen as running from bishop to superintendent to pastor. The convocation was a means of making certain that at the start of each four-year cycle the superintendents understood the denominational program, the special quadrennial emphasis if there was one, and the financial goals.

The first DS Convocation had been a kick-off rally for the Crusade for Christ in 1944, followed by a mid-quadrennium conference. There were two others for the Advance for Christ and His Church in 1948-52. The Commission on Promotion and Cultivation continued the series throughout its life; the last was in 1968. The Evangelical United Brethren used a similar plan.

A convocation was a combination pep rally, information channel and idea exchange. Networks were built and morale raised as superintendents, who sometimes felt isolated, met others who were doing the same work and facing the same problems. Programs featured sermons, speeches about the work of the church, small-group discussions, films and exhibits of resources.

The DS Convocation as an institution had two major problems. Not all superintendents were eager to learn about the general church program and its finances. What they wanted—especially those just beginning their terms—was coaching on *how to be* superintendent. But bishops saw the convocation as encroaching on their turf whenever it moved toward training for the superintendent's basic task.

Subsequently what had begun as a program-oriented convocation became an annual training session for newly appointed superintendents and directors of the Conference Council on Ministries, administered by the General Council on Ministries.

Leadership and Staff

Mohn, always bubbling with enthusiasm for the newest cause to be promoted, continued in charge until retiring at age seventy-two in 1960. He expected much of his staff, but no more than he demanded of himself. He had grown up before the era of the coffee break and resented that custom. An office legend concerned a meeting with several of his staff during which he needed some papers. He jabbed the buzzer for his secretary. No response. He exploded about how people were always on coffee break when you needed them. Hesitantly, Oscar Simpson ventured, "Dr. Mohn, it's past five o'clock and I think they've all gone home."

It was the same Mohn who gave his staff coffee mugs with "Back to Work" printed in the bottom. They were given in fun—but he meant it.

A young district superintendent in California had come to the attention of Bishop Martin and Mohn. His name was Howard Greenwalt. Reared on a farm in downstate Illinois, he was a graduate of Illinois College and Garrett Biblical Institute. Thinking he might be too liberal for rural Illinois, he opted to go west, serving churches in Nevada and northern California. At San Leandro he had carried out a major building project.

While superintendent of Central District of California-Nevada Conference, Greenwalt sensed a need for an instrument to help congregations evaluate their ministry. Not finding one, he designed his own. He called it the *Look-a-Graf*, and it found ready acceptance in the conference. Then it was described in *The Story* in 1955 and had some use in other areas.

As superintendent Greenwalt also created the district property book, a loose-leaf guide to every church building and parsonage to help new superintendents learn their district and to help them talk with pastors about prospective appointments.

Because of the key role of the superintendent in the strategy of the commission, Mohn invited Greenwalt to join the staff in the summer of 1956 with responsibility to develop field work with superintendents, but also to be business manager of the office. One of his first tasks was to develop the distribution plan for *The Methodist Story*, including a system to collect from every church the names and addresses of local lay officials who were entitled to free subscriptions.

To succeed the retiring Mohn as general secretary in 1960, the commission chose the Rev. Elliott L. Fisher, who had been a pastor and district superintendent in California and on the staff of the Division of National Missions in the Board of Missions. He continued Dr. Greenwalt as his associate.

In 1962 the commission joined other Methodist agencies in a move from downtown Chicago to suburban Evanston, where promotional offices continued until consolidation of UMCom offices in Nashville in 1986.

Bishop Donald Harvey Tippett, who had chaired TRAFCO, became president of the Commission on Promotion and Cultivation in 1964.

The next year Fisher suffered a fatal heart attack while standing in line at an airport in New York. In the trauma of the sudden loss of leadership, Greenwalt was named acting general secretary and after a few months was elected to the post. He continued through the duration of the commission as a separate agency and into the combined agency of United Methodist Communications.

Greenwalt developed the field staff, assigning responsibility by jurisdictions for them to speak in behalf of benevolences, conduct workshops, and offer training to district superintendents and other conference leaders in interpretation of the church program.

Clergy who were brought into the staff for field work were Alex Porteus from Florida and New York, the Rev. Arthur V. Long of Iowa, the Rev. Warren Jenkins of South Carolina, the Rev. Jun Jue of California, the Rev. R. Merrill Powers of the Northern Illinois Conference and the Rev. Frank Countryman, also of Northern Illinois. Dr. Powers was responsible for administration of a quadrennial program, 1964-68. The Rev. Nelson Stants from the Evangelical United Brethren side of the family joined the field staff in 1968.

Publications

Under Fisher and Greenwalt the work was organized into two departments: field staff and editorial department. First Greenwalt and then Long headed the field work. Maynard, who began as editor of *The Methodist Story*, was made editor of promotional materials in addition, and then headed the department as editorial director, with Shamblin promoted to editor of the magazine. Joretta Eppley and then Anna Marie Pritts were managing editors of the magazine under Shamblin. Later, in 1968, Ralph E. Baker took that title.

With the retirement of Simpson in 1964, the Rev. Earl Kenneth Wood came from conference public relations in Colorado as editor of promotional materials. Another writer/editor was Ruth D. Fuller. For a number of years Melvin L. Shepherd was a writer and production manager. Soon after the start of the magazine, Edward J. Mikula had been retained as a free-lance artist to do layout and illustrations. In a year or so he was asked to join the staff and to start an art department to meet all the agency's graphic design needs.

There was plenty of work for the artist and his associate. Through the years the World Service Leaflets were continued, although eventually it became too costly to publish one for every month. In 1959, 2,750,000 copies of each leaflet were printed.

By 1960 the commission's responsibility included promotion of World Service, the Interdenominational Co-operation Fund, the Advance and two special offerings. For each of those, posters and leaflets were standard tools for promotion. Samples of new materials and order forms were mailed quarterly to every pastor in the denomination.

Novelty items, such as coin boxes, mobiles and displays stretched the creativity of the staff. Since the mimeograph machine was the medium of choice in the parish, mimeo stencil insets were made for most of the promotions. Starting in 1967 there was a "Parish Paper Service," offering pre-cut stencils and reproduction proofs for offset printing. It contained news of the church and promotional information to be used as a page of a parish newsletter. This was created in California by Raymond Wilson, who originated the idea and published the service under contract until his death.

One of the creative firsts for the staff was a sound sheet—a light-weight plastic phonograph record, published as an insert in *The Methodist Story* in December 1965 in support of the Television-Radio Ministry Fund. It attracted attention in publishing and public relations circles and was repeated in behalf of several other funds.

Creative promotional tools included dramas, turnover charts, clocks, audio-cassette tapes and a tourist map locating church institutions and mission projects. The map went through several editions from 1959 to 1975 and appeared on thousands of bulletin boards and in glove compartments.

Millions of offering envelopes were distributed.

For many years the commission published a co-ordinated calendar of meetings. In 1968 a Program Calendar was introduced as an aid to local church program planning and a reminder of benevolences. It continues in 1990.

Changing Patterns

Through the years, patterns of funds to be promoted changed. Promotion of the World Service Fund was always a priority. Other apportioned funds, such as the Episcopal Fund and Interdenominational Co-operation Fund, required less promotion, though the latter called for interpretive effort whenever public attacks were made on ecumenical bodies—notably the World and National Councils of Churches.

Promotion of General Advance Specials was another major responsibility, shared with cultivation efforts of agencies that administered the funds. Successive General Conferences altered the names and timing of special days and the purposes of their offerings. The Week of Dedication in 1960 gave way to One Great Hour of Sharing, observed by a number of denominations to support overseas relief. The Fellowship of Suffering and Service always related to Worldwide Communion Sunday in October. After church union in 1968 the fellowship concept was phased out and the name was "World Communion Sunday Offering." By 1972 there were four Sundays with offerings to be promoted.

Emergency appeals were issued from time to time. Some, like the Bishops' Appeal for Korea already mentioned, were sanctioned by formal vote of the Council of Bishops and Council on World Service and Finance. Others, such as response to an earthquake in Chile or a hurricane in the Caribbean, were promoted as Advance Specials for the Methodist Committee on Overseas Relief, or in connection with the One Great Hour of Sharing.

After the Soviet invasion of Hungary in 1956 there were tens of thousands of displaced persons. For their relief and resettlement an appeal raised more than a million dollars in six months. Centerpiece of the promotion was Oscar Simpson's photo of a forlorn Hungarian child.

A Bishops' Appeal for Africa in 1961 raised $1.3 million for food, health services and leadership training in turbulent newly independent nations. Promotion was built around the famous talking drums that serve as the "jungle telegraph" of central Africa—one of which stood for many weeks in the Chicago office of the Commission on Promotion and Cultivation. To tell the story, pastors were provided with a poster, leaflets and a phonograph record that featured the sound of the talking drum and a message by Bishop Newell S. Booth of Africa. Several million offering envelopes in the shape of a talking drum were used.

The Story on the Screen

Audiovisuals were used for nearly all the promotions. Under the Commission on Promotion and Cultivation, the first motion picture was a stewardship film, *The Hidden Heart. See All the People* was made in 1962 for the Advance with Greenwalt as executive producer. That was followed by a World Service film, *And on the Eighth Day.*

Films came in growing numbers, most but not all produced by TRAFCO. Earl Wood was an active and creative film producer. One of his innovations was *With Banners Flying*, produced by video camera, a method now common but new at the time. Among other notable films were *Heart and Hands, In Any Language, Spaceship Earth, Do You Know My Name?, Candidly Speaking, Take Any Day,* and *Symbol of a Bell.*

Filmstrips and slide sets were widely used. And in 1971, to interpret the desperate plight of refugees from Bangladesh, a "Sight Sound Set" was created—a combination of audio cassette, colored slides and black-and-white photographs.

Field staff worked with conferences through many consultations and training sessions. Addresses were given and resources publicized. A number of conferences welcomed a plan called "Operation Understanding," which brought spokespersons from the general agencies in a design to have at least one guest speaker in every church of a district.

For promotion in the annual conference a co-operative filmstrip, *Where in the World Am I?*, was developed by Maynard and J. Fred Rowles of the TRAFCO staff. Through arrangements by the field staff, annual conference editions were made. Approximately half of the frames were "standard" pictures to represent World Service at the churchwide level, and the other half showed the benevolence program of the conference.

Pilot projects were done with Nebraska, Memphis and Western New York Conferences, and then it was offered to others with costs shared. After two years, when the project was phased out at the end of 1969, editions had been produced for fifteen conferences and 1,500 prints had been made of the filmstrips. Four conferences produced slide sets in a similar vein. *Where in the World Am I?* was replaced with a plan for co-operative financing of brochures. (The co-operative filmstrip concept was re-introduced later and continued until 1984, when it was again replaced by co-operative brochures.)

A new technology, Super-8mm films employing a cartridge-load system, was introduced at the 1968 District Superintendents' Convocation. Projectors were sold and agencies committed themselves to produce films in the format. However, Super-8 never really caught on.

The Cross and Flame

In the mid-1960s the forthcoming union of the EUB and Methodist Churches was a major topic. Howard Greenwalt was eager for the new church to have an appropriate insigne. The Evangelical United Brethren had one; Methodists never had. With Chicago artist Burton M. Cherry, Greenwalt had developed the "World Parish Cross," consisting of a golden cross in block style with a polar projection of the globe in red where the arms crossed.

He had offered it to the World Methodist Council in 1961 and the Methodist General Conference in 1964 to become an official symbol, but it was not accepted. So it was used in promotional work and was popular as a lapel pin.

As union neared, Greenwalt approached the Joint Commission on Union about a symbol for the new church. It was written into the *Discipline* that such an insigne should be created by and supervised by the Division of Interpretation. The staff assignment was given to Maynard and Mikula—the former to research and recommend content and the artist to do the design. The result was the Cross and Flame, now seen at United Methodist churches around the world and reproduced in bronze, glass and stone as well as in print.

Church Union, 1968

The Evangelical United Brethren Church had no direct counterpart to the Commission on Promotion and Cultivation. Promotional resources were created by the Council of Administration. Film resources from the National Council of Churches were used, and denominational productions were done either through its publishing house or the Council of Administration. The council produced an annual plan book for local churches.

The Council of Administration in 1955 began publishing a quarterly program resource for local churches, called *Spotlight*. Through joint staff work prior to the actual union, *Spotlight* was merged with the Methodist program journal so that at the Uniting Conference in Dallas, delegates had on their desks the first issue of *Methodist Story-Spotlight*. The following January the name was changed to *The Interpreter* (Chapter 13).

In the structure of the new denomination, the joint commission proposed a Program Council to bring more unity into the program operation of church agencies and to make the media of communication servants of the common program. One of the council's three divisions was for co-ordination, research and planning; the other two were communication agencies: TRAFCO and what was then called Division of Interpretation.

Under this arrangement, effective in 1968, Paul Church, as general secretary of the Program Council, was over the entire mix. Greenwalt became associate general secretary of the council with responsibility for the division. The work went on largely unchanged.

One significant change, however, was a clearcut understanding that the division had responsibility to interpret general church program—heretofore done mainly through the magazine. The Rev. Harold H. Hazenfield, who had been executive editor of church school publications in the Evangelical United Brethren Church, joined the carryover Methodist staff with the title editor of program materials. Dr. Hazenfield prepared separate materials, such as the Program Calendar and Tourist Map, and also supervised program content for *The Interpreter*. He made a unique contribution to the entire program during the ten years until his retirement.

Also in 1968 the magazine staff moved from Evanston to Dayton, Ohio, in the former EUB office building. Other functions of the Division of Interpretation, including the office of the associate general secretary, continued in the Evanston offices formerly used by the Commission on Promotion and Cultivation.

The structure of 1968 brought more unity to communication agencies than had existed in The Methodist Church. The Structure Study Commission of 1968-72 envisaged even more. It proposed a plan, reminiscent of the 1952 idea, that would have combined the Division of Interpretation, TRAFCO, United Methodist Information, and the United Methodist Publishing House. It came close to prevailing, but General Conference members feared the problems of linking a self-supporting, non-subsidized agency (the publishing house), with communication work supported by benevolence funds.

The 1972 General Conference created the Joint Committee on Communications, quickly given the name United Methodist Communications for popular use.

Greenwalt was reluctant about the new scheme, because he believed promotional work was in a stronger position if detached. Moreover, he felt that some of the church's professional communicators tended to downgrade promotion. But many of the

Division of Interpretation staff, daily involved in use of all media of communication, welcomed the development. As a matter of fact, the 1968 *Book of Discipline* instructed the promotion agency to "employ all available means of communication."

Charged to promote benevolence giving with goals of more than $60,000,000 a year among 40,000 churches with 10,500,000 members, the staff went into the new agency, soon identified as "Division of Program and Benevolence Interpretation."

·7·

Seeing Communication Whole

In 1940 when Methodist Information opened for business, the Evangelical Church and the Church of the United Brethren in Christ were separate denominations.

Both churches were of American origin, in theology and organization very like the Methodists. While begun in the eighteenth century among German settlers in Pennsylvania and Maryland, by 1940 they had long been English-speaking, middle-of-the-road denominations. They had spread through the eastern, midwestern and western states.

In November of 1946 at Johnstown, Pennsylvania, the two joined as the Evangelical United Brethren Church, often referred to as EUB. This denomination combined with The Methodist Church in 1968 to form The United Methodist Church.

As noted in Chapter 2, during the nineteenth century the Evangelicals and United Brethren moved into the mass media through print. They published books, newspapers and magazines in German and English. By 1946 the primary periodical of the Evangelical Church was the *Evangelical Messenger*, with a circulation of 23,000, and the United Brethren had the *Religious Telescope* with 27,000. These were soon combined into the weekly *Telescope-Messenger* with the Rev. Joe Willard Krecker as editor.

The newly merged denomination in 1946 had nearly three-quarters of a million members. The *Telescope-Messenger*, after beginning with a list of 50,000, was down to 42,000 by 1950, but later moved up to 49,000 (1958-61). *Builders*, a popular youth magazine edited by the Rev. Raymond M. Veh, had circulation of 100,000.

In 1964 the *Telescope-Messenger*, by then bi-weekly, and a family magazine, *Our Home*, were replaced by the slick-paper semi-monthly *Church and Home*. Krecker was editor and his associate was a young clergyman with a doctorate in pastoral counseling and an interest in audiovisuals, who since 1959 had been editor of adult publications in church-school literature for the Board of Publication. He was Curtis A. Chambers, destined to become the first general secretary of United Methodist Communications. Lee A. Ranck was managing editor, beginning a long editorial career in the EUB and United Methodist Churches.

Church and Home enjoyed phenomenal success with a starting circulation of 264,000 and maintained well above 200,000. This was achieved with an all-family plan that encouraged churches to subscribe for all their member homes. In 1966 there were 232,000 subscribers among 355,000 families, 65 percent saturation—a record without parallel among Protestant publications of the United States. In 1967, with Dr. Chambers as executive editor, it switched to monthly frequency. After the union of 1968 it was combined with the Methodist *Together*. Chambers joined the general church periodicals staff and was editor of *Together* 1969-72, then editorial director.

A program journal, *Spotlight* (Chapter 13), was begun in 1955 by three agencies and later published by the Program Council.

Communication Responsibilities

While strong in publishing, the Evangelical United Brethren Church did not at first have structural units assigned to communication tasks. What was done in the area was accomplished independently by the Board of Missions, Board of Christian Education and Board of Evangelism. In time these isolated communication activities came to be co-ordinated by the Council of Administration, a central authority symbolic of the denomination's commitment to holistic administration and program.

The council administered and promoted the Mission and Benevolence Budget (after 1962, Christian Service Fund); promoted special days and their offerings; and used tracts, films and filmstrips to educate church members in stewardship. It sponsored convocations of conference superintendents. While the council's major responsibilities were in administration, its promotional work was parallel to the Methodist Commission on Promotion and Cultivation.

In 1946 responsibility for audiovisuals was assigned to the Board of Christian Education, with distribution by the Board of Publication. A few productions were done also by the Board of Missions and Board of Evangelism. While there were not many original EUB productions, the Board of Education was a party to joint productions through the Protestant Film Commission, later Broadcasting and Film Commission of the National Council of Churches. Chambers chaired the board's Audiovisual Committee 1960-64.

Within the Council of Administration a logo for the EUB denomination was created and made official by the 1958 General Conference. It was the work of the Rev. Ralph M. Holdeman, executive secretary of the Board of Evangelism and also a graphic artist and sculptor. (The insigne consisted of the church name surrounding a plain Latin cross and a prominent handclasp, symbolizing the famous 1767 meeting in a Pennsylvania barn between Martin Boehm and Philip William Otterbein. The latter said, *"Wir sind Brueder"*—"We are brethren"—inspiring the name for the United Brethren.)

For major church meetings, particularly General Conference every four years, persons with communication skills were co-opted from the staffs of church agencies. By 1954 General Conference arrangements included a Committee on Radio and Television headed by the Rev. (later Bishop) Reuben H. Mueller, and a Committee on Ushering, Bookstore and Audio-visual Displays, led by L. L. Huffman, head of Otterbein Press.

Dr. Veh, the *Builders* editor, was publicity-minded and led in a bigger public relations effort for the 1958 General Conference. He had become acquainted with Chambers, then a pastor in Harrisburg, Pennsylvania, and invited him to write a regular column for *Builders*. Chambers at the time chaired a broadcast committee for the local council of churches and was on a committee administering a trust fund to sponsor events to promote use of media in churches and other organizations in the county. For the General Conference, meeting in Harrisburg, Veh undertook to do press relations himself and asked Chambers to work with radio and television.

In preparation, Chambers took training from Charles H. Schmitz of the Broadcasting and Film Commission, National Council of Churches, talked with communication officers of several denominations, and observed public relations activities at a Lutheran meeting. Veh had good success with advance publicity and news coverage during the conference. Chambers generated interview and program possibilities and, as he put it, "peddled them around to the stations." A number of broadcasts resulted.

The 1958 results were encouraging enough that the Veh-Chambers team did public relations for the 1962 General Conference in Grand Rapids, Michigan.

Committee on Communication

As experience demonstrated need for a more intentional approach to communication, the Council of Administration during the quadrennium 1958-62 formed a Committee on Communication. The committee drew personnel from the church's boards and commissions, all of which were headquartered in one building in Dayton, Ohio. There were three subcommittees: Public Information, Audiovisual Co-ordination, and Radio-TV Ministry.

The idea came from the Rev. Paul V. Church, who in 1960 was elected executive secretary of the Council of Administration. While a pastor and later conference superintendent in Illinois, Dr. Church had displayed an interest in communication. As a pastor he used audiovisuals and created some of his own. More than his

70

predecessors in the Council of Administration, he was aware of the potential communications offered the church, and he wanted to see more effective work.

The Committee on Communication was to co-ordinate communication activity being developed—or at least dreamed about—in the staffs of EUB program boards. There was interest on the part of the Rev. E. Craig Brandenburg and the Rev. Warren J. Hartman in education and Ralph Holdeman and the Rev. John R. Knecht in evangelism. Knecht, a young minister from Indiana (later a seminary president), was urging a national EUB radio program.

The concept of the Communication Committee was fine, but first results meager. To the 1962 General Conference the Council of Administration reported: "Since this committee is . . . limited in its budget it has been able to do little more than meet and lay some plans for the new quadrennium." It was promised that the committee would correlate the present work done by boards in these areas and "initiate new program to fill a gap in the life of our church."

In 1961 the Rev. (later bishop) Wayne K. Clymer, dean of Evangelical Theological Seminary, was placed on network radio as summer replacement for Norman Vincent Peale on *The Art of Living*.

In the next four years, as a Department of Communication in the Council of Administration, the co-opted staff pursued the holistic concept of communication, but with a budget of only $10,000 a year. Church, as executive secretary of the council, was also department director, and Chambers was secretary. The Rev. Donald R. Lantz, a writer and producer for Family Films in Hollywood, chaired the department's committee, which was made up of agency staff persons and representatives from various parts of the church. Radio/TV work was done through the National Council of Churches, and there was some work to promote utilization of audiovisuals. A few press releases were issued.

During 1965 a series of meetings was held with the leadership of annual conference departments of communication. It was reported that most were publishing newspapers and some were effective with audiovisual libraries. Only a few were working in public information. "On the whole," it was reported in 1966, "much remains to be done in our annual conferences if we are going to begin to catch up in this important field."

By then, of course, planning toward the union of 1968 was well under way.

Church Union Comes

In 1966 the regular Evangelical United Brethren General Conference convened in Chicago and an adjourned session of the Methodist General Conference met at the same time—both in the Conrad Hilton Hotel. Chambers had been asked to head up EUB public relations. Arthur West of Methodist Information and Harry Spencer of TRAFCO were planning the Methodist news operation. Consulting with one another, they agreed on a combined effort with Chambers as general chairman and West and Spencer working in their specialties. Additional staff were provided by each church. Unknowingly, they arrived at an arrangement that presaged future staff relationships in United Methodist Communications.

The concept of program co-ordination under a council was a major contribution of the EUB church to the structure of the united church. A Program Council, first authorized in 1962, was developed as a place where EUB agency staff could co-ordinate their programs. It functioned within the Council of Administration under Church's leadership.

A Joint Commission on Church Union developed the design for the united church, and Chambers became a member of it, serving as co-editor (with Emory S. Bucke, book editor in the Methodist Publishing House) of the first *Book of Discipline*. The Plan of Union built upon the concept of program co-ordination with unified communications related to it. The plan, when adopted, established a Program Council with three divisions: Co-ordination, Research and Planning; Television, Radio and Film Communication; and Interpretation. The latter two brought staff and functions from their Methodist predecessors.

General secretary of the United Methodist Program Council was

72

Dr. Church. In this post he was top administrator for the two communication units. (Relationships with the public media remained independent as United Methodist Information.) Two other staff persons came from EUB agencies into the Division of Interpretation in 1968. The Rev. Harold H. Hazenfield, who had headed the editorial staff for all EUB church school literature as executive editor, became editor of program materials. The Rev. Nelson E. Stants, who had assumed responsibility for stewardship cultivation in 1965, became one of the division's field representatives.

Thus began organized communications in the united church. The EUBs contributed a holistic concept and the Methodists contributed staff and ongoing program. Further unity in communications was yet to come in the restructure in 1972.

·8·

Working Together

*T*he crucial step in unifying the communication functions in The United Methodist Church came with the General Conference of 1972. But it was not until 1976 that the church declared why.

The 1976 *Book of Discipline* stated the purpose for a united communication agency:

> As United Methodists, our theological understanding obligates us, as members of the Body of Christ, to communicate our faith by speaking and listening to persons both within and outside the Church throughout the world, and to utilize all appropriate means of communication.

The statement acknowledged that every Christian and every unit of the church are under obligation to communicate the faith, adding that certain functions were assigned to United Methodist Communications "to be performed in behalf of all."

The preamble to state the purpose of communication was placed in the *Discipline* by the General Conference at the request of the communication agency—a result of theological studies during the quadrennium.

Instructions in the *Discipline* for the predecessor communication agencies had been bureaucratic. The task had been seen largely as co-ordination or service to some other church agency. But now communication was seen as an essential function of the Christian faith, employing "all appropriate means" (media).

Although the EUB experience (Chapter 7) and the first four years in the united church, 1968-72, had moved toward a holistic approach to communication, the decision at the 1972 General Conference did not come easily.

A four-year study of the church's administrative structure, ordered by the Uniting Conference, recommended merging three communication units with the United Methodist Publishing House. The idea was supported by many, but also opposed—largely on grounds that it would combine a self-supporting quasi-commercial corporation with subsidized units. The General Conference found one of its legislative committees reporting favorably on that plan, while another recommended a plan that had been developed by the Program Council. By 535-406 the conference chose the latter.

What was created was a "Joint Committee on Communications"—"joint" because the governing body was composed of ten members of the General Council on Ministries and ten members of the General Council on Finance and Administration, plus ten at-large elected by the first twenty. The staff and functions came from United Methodist Information, the Division of Interpretation and the Division of Television, Radio and Film Communication. Unification was accomplished, but the function in 1972 was "to serve the General Council on Ministries and the general boards . . . to meet their communication needs."

Chambers Is Elected

The first meeting of the Joint Committee chose as its chair Thomas P. Moore, a radio station owner-operator from Bucyrus, Ohio. It was agreed that, while search for an executive secretary went on, the now-joined units would function as before under existing leadership. The Rev. Paul V. Church, general secretary of the General Council on Ministries (formerly Program Council), would double as interim chief executive.

By May of 1973, the Joint Committee's search committee made a recommendation, out of forty candidates, that was adopted unanimously by the full committee. The nominee: the Rev. Curtis A. Chambers.

Dr. Chambers had been editor of *Together*, a general interest magazine published by the United Methodist Publishing House. In 1972 he became editorial director for *Together* and a journal for clergy, *Christian Advocate*. Before church union he had been executive editor of the Evangelical United Brethren Church's popular *Church and Home* (Chapter 7).

Ohio born and educated at Marion College there, Chambers studied at the conservative Asbury Theological Seminary (bachelor of divinity, 1950) and liberal Oberlin Graduate School of Theology (post-graduate study 1951-53). Later he earned master's and doctor's degrees at Temple University. He was ordained by the Evangelical United Brethren Church in 1954 and served pastorates in Ohio and Pennsylvania. As a pastor he pursued interests in communications, especially audiovisuals.

In 1959 Chambers became editor of adult publications in church-school literature for the EUB Board of Publication. He moved to *Church and Home* in 1963 as associate editor and in 1967 became executive editor, continuing until the magazine's merger with *Together* in 1969. At General Conferences he directed radio-television coverage in 1958 and 1962 and chaired the entire communication operation in 1966. He chaired National Council of Churches committees on audiovisual and educational media 1962-66.

Building a Staff

Assuming office in the fall of 1973, Chambers presided over a first staff meeting that included several unsuccessful candidates for his job. By personal philosophy and experience in the EUB Church he was committed to a holistic approach to communication. The staff he led came from units with long history as independent agencies, and the individuals, while in principle committed to seeing communication whole, prized independence in decision making. And they had turf to protect.

Chambers and Moore sought to make it truly a unified agency, more than the sum of its three predecessors. Aided by a structure committee, they planned four divisions that did not follow lines of the previous agencies. The divisions: Public Media; Production and Distribution; Program and Benevolence Interpretation (P&BI); and Research, Education and Liaison (REAL). The former United Methodist Information became a department within the Division of Public Media. Former TRAFCO responsibilities were split between two divisions. The old Division of Interpretation remained largely intact, but gave up functions in the areas of distribution and field service.

The first three divisions were headed, respectively, by the Rev. Arthur West, the Rev. Harry C. Spencer and the Rev. Howard Greenwalt. The fourth, which never really became a division, was led by the Rev. Gene W. Carter as acting head, but in 1975 it was discontinued, with most of its staff and functions going into an Office of Communication Education and Field Service.

Agency headquarters were established in Dayton, Ohio, because of a close relationship to the General Council on Ministries. Offices of Chambers, Carter and *The Interpreter* were in the Dayton building that had been erected as EUB Church headquarters. Other offices were continued in Nashville, New York, Washington and Evanston.

In October 1973 Dr. Spencer retired. His successor as associate executive secretary for Production and Distribution was James Campbell. Campbell had joined the TRAFCO staff in 1959 as associate director of utilization and had moved through several positions to assistant general secretary for media resources. Previously he had been a pastor in Mississippi and South Carolina and had experience in radio, television and audiovisuals.

In the early years, Joe W. Davis, who had long served with TRAFCO, was financial officer. After his disability retirement he was succeeded in 1976 by Anna L. Conley.

When Arthur West retired in 1975, Nelson Price was moved up to head the Public Media Division. Like Campbell, he had joined the TRAFCO staff in 1959. Iowa born, he moved from his Morningside College graduation in 1951 to directing public relations for the Indiana Area in 1952. After five years he moved to Chicago to do public relations for the Rock River Conference.

77

At TRAFCO Price began training conference committees and community production teams for the popular *Talk Back* TV show. He also prepared print materials, including a newsletter. In 1961 he was made director of a production unit. He became a producer, most notably of the *Breakthru* television series. In 1964 he became assistant general secretary and two years later was sent to the New York office. There he related to broadcast media and continued producing. He was producer of *Night Call*, the unique national call-in radio program. He headed the broadcast section of the division from its creation until becoming associate general secretary.

In 1974 Martha Man came from Dallas, where she had been editor of religion news for the *Times-Herald*, to be news writer in New York. West had continued to direct the news service while heading the division. When Price became associate general secretary, he continued to direct the broadcast section and he named Man director of News Service.

As a name for popular usage the Joint Committee on Communications voted in May 1973 to use "United Methodist Communications." It was made official by the *Discipline* of 1976. At first it was abbreviated as UMC, but because "UMC" often was used to mean "United Methodist Church," the official acronym in 1980 became "UMCom"—preferred pronunciation, "EU-EM-COM."

Meanwhile the Joint Committee approach was found inadequate—in part because of the burden placed upon persons already members of the two major councils and because of a perceived conflict of interest. But especially, a governing board with a primary interest in communication was desired to represent sections of the church and to include specialists in the various media. In 1980 the General Commission on Communication was created, and the title of the chief executive was changed to general secretary, reflecting a new status.

New Ideas

The two quadrenniums from 1972 to 1980 were years of consolidating the agency, determining its proper role, integrating the staff, and developing loyalties to the unified agency. They were also exciting years, a time of many innovations.

Field staff had picked up strong signals that the church needed some kind of "hot line" to answer questions, register complaints and counter rumors. A staff team developed what was to be called InfoServ (Chapter 9). The consultant who helped bring InfoServ from idea to reality was Peggy J. West, a former college English teacher with a fresh Ph.D., who in 1979 returned to UMCom to head the Division of Production and Distribution after Campbell resigned to pursue personal business interests.

Film distribution was begun in 1975 as United Methodist Film Service (Chapter 11).

The old TRAFCO building at 1525 McGavock Street, Nashville, was overcrowded by new work, and a nearby residence-turned-store was converted for InfoServ. But the old studios continued to turn out new productions.

An Easter film, *One Who Was There*, was produced in 1978, with Donald Hughes as director. The film tells the story of one of the witnesses to the Resurrection, Mary Magdalene, and the changes that came to her life from the influence of the Christ. It starred two well-known Hollywood figures: Maureen O'Sullivan and her daughter, Tisa Farrow, as Mary at different ages.

A New Building

Not only was the Nashville building crowded; the old TRAFCO questions of function and location never went away. Chambers led the agency in a study of location strategy. The rationale for offices in five cities had been to have staff in places where United Methodist general agencies were located. That reasoning was sustained, and the governing commission determined to keep all locations, keep the headquarters in Dayton and erect a new building in Nashville with studio and technical facilities for film and video production.

An agency building committee struggled with problems of location in Nashville, finance and sale of the old building. Finally, on September 25, 1979, ground was broken in an urban redevelopment area. After two years of construction, the staff of the Division of Production and Distribution and related offices moved in December 1980. The new building cost $2.2 million, had 34,000 square feet of space and contained three studios: film/video, radio and music.

It was the first new United Methodist agency building in twenty years. Key persons in making it happen—along with Chambers as general secretary and Charles J. Cappleman as chair of the Joint Committee on Communications—were Thomas Moore, who headed the building committee; Dr. Peggy West, whose staff would use the facilities; Peggy W. Welshans, financial officer for UMCom; and Anton (Tony) Pilversack, whose experience helped shape building design to production and distribution needs.

The new building enhanced UMCom's production capabilities. It also enlarged opportunity for Kingswood Productions—the tax-paying company (Chapter 5) that for years had minimized losses by renting out TRAFCO and UMCom studios for commercial use at hours not required for church productions.

More to Promote

Meanwhile the Division of Program and Benevolence Interpretation was busy promoting an ever-larger benevolence program— $67.5 million in 1978. While *The Interpreter* and printed leaflets and posters continued to be mainstays of promotional work, the division used many media. Notable promotional tools were the brochure *What Happens to All that Money?* and the World Service film *A Part of Something Big*. An annual program calendar, also containing promotional helps, was issued, and the United Methodist Tourist Map appeared in a 1975 edition locating 1,300 institutions and points of interest.

A new assignment came to P&BI in 1976, when for the first time the General Conference adopted "missional priorities"—three of them. They were Evangelism, World Hunger and the Ethnic Minority Local Church. The priorities involved raising extra dollars and interpreting vital programs, and the division had major responsibilities.

The Parish Paper Service, begun by the Commission on Promotion and Cultivation, continued under contract with Raymond Wilson (Chapter 6). The division marketed a book about parish newsletters by Wilson, who reasoned that more persons read them than any other church periodicals. At one point the service was used by 2,000 churches, but it never reached its circulation goals and was discontinued upon Wilson's death in the late 1970s.

The quadrenniums 1981-84 and 1985-88 had single missional priorities which centered on ethnic minority local churches. The P&BI Division devoted major energies to training leaders and producing resources for the programs.

The Periodicals Study

Stung by the decision of the United Methodist Publishing House in 1975 to discontinue *United Methodists Today*, which had briefly replaced *Together*, the General Council on Ministries asked UMCom to conduct a "national periodical publications study." With deadlines compressed to get a report before the 1976 General Conference, the team carried out a massive study in less than six months. The team consisted of six from UMCom, one from the General Council on Ministries and two from the publishing house.

The report was made to the Joint Committee on Communications in the fall of 1975, then to the General Council on Ministries, and finally the General Conference. It recommended a unified approach to communications for the entire denomination at all levels, to be called a Comprehensive Communication System. Some persons in general agencies felt it signaled encroachment by UMCom on their freedom to use the media. Others feared the cost of radio and television ministries. A proposal to restore a churchwide general periodical was dropped.

The plan approved by UMCom and GCOM carried a price of $1.3 million a year in new money. Scaled down to $659,000 it nevertheless was rejected twice by the Council on Finance and Administration. But at the 1976 General Conference, after much struggle and a dramatic solo fight on the floor by Robert Cheyne, the conference voted an annual fund of $600,000 for mass communications (more in Chapter 10).

Major components of the comprehensive plan were implemented. Changes were made in *The Interpreter*. Agency communicators and conference representatives began to meet regularly with UMCom staff to share information and plan together. The principle of "wholesaling" services to annual conferences (for example, training local persons for communications) was accepted.

Another innovation by the 1976 General Conference was provision for a coordinator of communications in the local church. UMCom took steps to provide resources and training.

Changes in Staff

Howard Greenwalt, who had led the former Division of Interpretation in the Program Council, continued as associate general secretary for the Division of Program and Benevolence Interpretation until 1977. In June of that year he was succeeded by the Rev. Readus J. Watkins, superintendent of Hudson West District in the New York Annual Conference. Previously Dr. Watkins had been a pastor in New York and New England and director of field services for the New York City Society (an urban ministry). For a time he directed the guidance and counseling department and was dean of the chapel at the University of Ghana in Africa.

Peggy West, who became associate general secretary for the Division of Production and Distribution in 1979, was reared in Arkansas. She received her bachelor's degree from Tulane University, a master's from Louisiana State, and a Ph.D. from the University of Arkansas. She worked as an editor, a librarian, and instructor in English, coming to Nashville in 1968 to teach English at Fisk University. After helping establish InfoServ, she worked as a free-lance consultant before returning to UMCom.

Also joining staff in 1979 was the Rev. Donald E. Collier, who came as assistant general secretary in the Division of Program and Benevolence Interpretation and in 1985, on the resignation of Dr. Watkins, succeeded him as associate general secretary. Collier was educated at Ohio Wesleyan University and Yale Divinity School and was ordained elder by New York Conference in 1960. After four pastorates in New York communities, he spent six years as associate program director for the conference. Then he was pastor of First Church, Meriden, Connecticut, 1974-79. He had developed skills in Christian education.

After 21 years in the Division of Program and Benevolence Interpretation and its predecessors, Maynard in 1977 took a newly created post as assistant to Chambers for research, planning and general administrative assistance. On his retirement, the position was taken in 1985 by Newtonia Harris Coleman, who had served on the staff of general periodicals for the Publishing House and was editor of *Now*, the newspaper of Black Methodists for Church Renewal. Her duties were expanded to include personnel, and the title was raised to associate general secretary.

Treasurer and chief financial officer has been Peggy W. Welshans, who joined the staff in 1977. Educated at the University of Tennessee and Memphis State University, she came to UMCom from an auditor's job with the state of Tennessee and received her CPA (certified public accountant) shortly after joining the staff. Her management and negotiating skills brought the agency through tight spots, notably in financing the new building and handling the financial crisis of the early 1980s.

General secretaries often say that their agencies consist of the people who do the work. That is true of United Methodist Communications. Among the names not mentioned elsewhere that deserve to be recorded for the years from 1972 to 1989 are the following:

General Administration—Betty J. Van Dyke, secretary and administrative assistant to the general secretary 1973-89; Anne Carey, her successor; Mary Glasgow, 35-year veteran in a number of positions; Sherri Thiel in finance; Brenda Blanton Lane, who lost her life by murder in 1985 shortly after starting work in public relations.

Division of Production and Distribution—Wayne Smith, Eryea Thompson, Harry Leake, Suzy Loftis Heydel, Nancy Jackson, Andrew Holt, Ronny Perry, Lafayette Richardson, William Dale, Dixie Parman, Bo Highfill and Phil Arnold.

Division of Public Media—Lee Parkinson, Jeff Weber, Stanley Nelson, Margaret Gothard, Jane Blocker, Kathleen H. Dale, Ascension Day and Robert Woods.

Division of Program and Benevolence Interpretation—Donald B. Moyer (editorial director when he was murdered in 1980 for motives and by a person unknown), Eleanor Knudsen, Charles Hightower, Donah Burgess, Ruth H. Jewett, Tim Spacek, Eddie Robinson, Phyllis Eggenberger, Orville D. Hinkle and Elsie Cunningham.

The deaths of Don Moyer and Brenda Lane were devastating to family and friends, deprived the agency of talented communication professionals and had traumatic impact on the staff.

A Startling Proposal

After elections of 1976, Tom Moore, who had guided UMCom through its formative years, was no longer a member of the Joint Committee on Communications. Elected as new chairman was a broadcasting executive whom UMCom first came to know in one of the three round tables that were part of the Periodical Publications Study. He was Charles J. Cappleman, a vice president of CBS and manager of its vast Television City studios in Los Angeles.

In 1978 Cappleman electrified committee members at the annual meeting when he called for a bold approach to television by the church. Why not, he challenged, own a television station? He often declared that "a television station license is a license to print money" and his dream was that a commercial station, operated on Christian principles in its programming and advertising, could produce programs for use elsewhere and earn money to finance United Methodist television on a national scale.

After much debate and 1980 General Conference action, a campaign for $25 million for Television Presence and Ministry was launched (Chapter 10). Despite a dramatic beginning, the campaign failed to win support and was called off, leaving the agency with a million-dollar debt. It was a financial disaster for UMCom. Not only was there not money for a TV station or new programming; the budget had to be rolled back to make payments on the debt. Programs were cancelled, and eleven staff positions were abolished. The successful radio program *Connection* (Chapter 10) was dropped, and communication education was curtailed abruptly.

plate 1

The UMCom Story in Pictures

All photos unless otherwise credited are from United Methodist Communications Archives.

W. W. Reid (center at the table), pioneer church communicator, shares a proper breakfast in the African bush with missionaries A. H. Klebsattel (left) and Newell S. Booth (later bishop). The photo was made about 1939 in Angola, where Reid went to write for the Board of Missions.— *Photo courtesy of General Board of Global Ministries*

In 1944 the *Christian Advocate* pictured the staff of Methodist Information: Ralph W. Stoody (in circle), director; Maud Turpin, Nashville manager; and George B. Ahn, Jr., Chicago manager.

plate 2

Reporters who covered the 1944 General Conference in Kansas City autographed this photo of the conference press room. Ralph W. Stoody, Methodist Information director, sits at desk in the back corner., and other staff are Maud Turpin, George B. Ahn, Jr., and Mary James (Duner).

Maud Turpin (at left behind counter) presides over a literature room for a women's gathering in the early 1940s.

plate 3

Press room staff for the 1952 Methodist General Conference in San Francisco includes (top) O. B. Fanning and (left to right) Charlotte O'Neal, Nadine Callahan, Ralph W. Stoody and Arthur West.

Among reporters covering the 1952 General Conference are (left to right) Bob Bell, Jr., Nashville *Banner*; Bill Bechtel, Milwaukee *Journal*; and Willmar Thorkelson, Minneapolis *Star*.

plate 4

Ethel Williams of the Nashville Methodist Information office is surrounded by clippings from newspaper coverage of the 1953 World Convocation on Evangelism. Convened in Philadelphia, it celebrated the 250th anniversary of John Wesley's birth.

When Methodist Information held its first national staff gathering at St. Simon's Island, Georgia, in 1953, most of the participants arrived in Brunswick by train. The mayors of Brunswick and the Golden Isles (left) welcome the group by offering keys to their cities to Ralph Stoody (center) and Arthur West (far right).—*Photo courtesy of Arthur West*

plate 5

A 1957 Methodist Information photo shows (seated left to right) Bishop Richard C. Raines, chairman; Ralph W. Stoody, general secretary; and (standing) Daniel Ridout, representative to the Negro press; and regional managers: Arthur West, Chicago; O. B. Fanning, Washington; and William M. Hearn, Nashville.

Snapped during a celebrated confrontation over freedom of access by the press are Arthur West (left) and W. A. Visser 't Hooft, general secretary of the World Council of Churches. The incident occurred during the WCC Assembly in Evanston, Illinois, in 1954.—*Photo courtesy of Arthur West*

plate 6

Writers work in the press room of the 1960 General Conference in Denver.

Press covering the annual meeting of the Board of Education in 1961 are (left to right) William M. Hearn, Methodist Information; A. C. Holler, South Carolina; Warren Carberg, New England; Ewing Wayland, Arkansas; Robert Lear, Methodist Information; and Carl Keightley, Texas.

plate 7

A child stars in the 1961 film on church public relations, *As Others See Us.* The film was made for Methodist Information by TRAFCO.

In the press room for the 1964 General Conference at Pittsburgh, George Dugan of the New York *Times* talks with (right) Margaret Donaldson, public relations director for the New York Episcopal Area. At left is Margaret Vance, a reporter from Newark, New Jersey.—*Photo courtesy of Robert Lear*

plate 8

A Methodist Information staff portrait made in St. Louis in 1964 includes (left to right) Charlotte O'Neal, William Hearn, Winston H. Taylor, Arthur West and Robert Lear.

Ralph W. Stoody gives an acknowledgment speech at a dinner honoring his retirement during the 1964 General Conference.

This United Methodist Information photo in the early 1970s includes (left to right) Thomas S. McAnally, Winston H. Taylor, Charlotte O'Neal, Arthur West and Leonard M. Perryman.—*Photo courtesy of Arthur West*

plate 9

A few days after the 1952 General Conference, the Radio and Film Commission met to elect officers and its first full-time staff. Pictured are (left to right) Bishop Donald H. Tippett, chairman; Howard E. Tower, associate executive secretary; and Harry C. Spencer, executive secretary.

An early and long-lasting accomplishment in film production was *John Wesley*, created by TRAF-CO and the Rank organization in England. In the title role, Leonard Sachs here reenacts Wesley's bold venture into field preaching.

plate 10

Sarah Cannon, who as Minnie Pearl is a well-known comedian on the country music circuit, is a lifelong United Methodist and friend of UMCom. In the 1950s she took part in a television production for children, and she has participated in numerous TRAF-CO and UMCom productions and events in subsequent years.

Encouraging use of audiovisuals was an important part of the work of the Radio and Film Commission and TRAFCO. Here Howard Tower demonstrates use of a motion picture projector.

plate 11

A bulky camera and microphone on a boom were standard tools for making films in the 1950s. The actor portrays a harried businessman in "Pressure" for the *Talk Back* series.

An elaborate set—one of many constructed in Studio A at the 1525 McGavock Street address—is used to film dramas for local church use and for television.

plate 12

Equipment surrounds a panel reacting to one of the films in the *Talk Back* TV series.

A youthful Patty Duke appeared in TRAFCO's television programming. She is seen here with actress Anne Ives in "Talking Hands," a program in the *Breakthru* series for children.

plate 13

A feature of the *Breakthru* TV series in the early 1960s was a panel of children to react to a filmed drama posing a moral dilemma. Live telecasts of local panels were the norm, but as backup there were filmed panels. Gene Atkins works with four children in the studio for filming in both pictures.

On location for the film, *Run Away Home*, John Clayton directs, with Ernest Allen at the camera.

plate 14

After the Commission on Promotion and Cultivation was formed in 1952, it tackled its assignment of co-ordinating promotional publications of various church agencies. Here a committee of the commission meets with promotional staff persons of the boards.

E. Harold Mohn, general secretary of the Commission on Promotion and Cultivation, addresses the 1957 District Superintendents' Convocation in Chicago.

plate 15

With their exhibit at the 1956 General Conference in Minneapolis are Bishop William C. Martin (left), president of the Commission on Promotion and Cultivation, and E. Harold Mohn, general secretary.

A meeting of the Commission on Promotion and Cultivation in Chicago in July 1956 includes E. Harold Mohn, general secretary, standing at the board. In center at the head table is Bishop William C. Martin, president.

plate 16

From 1952 to 1962 administrative offices of the Commission on Promotion and Cultivation were at 740 Rush Street, Chicago.

In 1958 the service department at 740 Rush Street was busy sending out materials published by the Commission on Promotion and Cultivation.

plate 17

In pre-computer days, maintaining circulation records was a manual operation. Shown is Ethel Hintz who headed the team responsible for files of *The Methodist Story*.

Pictured is the *Methodist Tourist Map*, a popular promotional tool for almost twenty years. It located institutions and points of interest. The first of its editions was published in 1959, and the last showed United Methodist places in 1975.

plate 18

An original oratorio, *The Invisible Fire*, is presented at the 1960 General Conference in Denver by the Commission on Promotion and Cultivation in partnership with general agencies of the denomination.

The planning committee for the 1960 District Superintendents' Convocation includes (left to right) Offie L. Hathaway; Herst Griffis; Walter Hazzard; Ray Ragsdale, committee chair; Elliott L. Fisher, general secretary; Theodore Mayer; and H. H. Luetzow.

plate 19

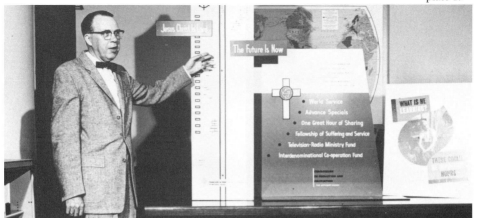

An exhibit for the quadrennial theme "The Future Is Now," created by the Commission on Promotion and Cultivation, is shown by Elliott L. Fisher, general secretary.

The promotional office's exhibit at the 1960 General Conference in Denver features a lounge area for delegates.

Bishop William C. Martin, who presided over the Commission on Promotion and Cultivation for twelve years, is honored at his retirement in 1964. From left to right are Edward J. Mikula, art director, who created a portrait of the bishop; Mrs. Martin; Bishop Martin; Eugene L. Smith of the Board of Missions; and Elliott L. Fisher.

plate 20

Table discussion is a feature of the District Superintendents' Convocation in 1964. In this group is R. Merrill Powers (foreground, third from left) of the commission staff.

The District Superintendents' Convocation of 1964 introduces the quadrennial theme "One Witness in One World."

plate 21

A table-top display was created by the Commission on Promotion and Cultivation for use in annual conferences. R. Merrill Powers (second from left) and Elliott L. Fisher (second from right) of the commission staff are among those pictured.

Staff of *The Methodist Story* view cover art for the issue of October 1957: (standing, left to right) Darrell R. Shamblin, managing editor; Edwin H. Maynard, editor; Oscar L. Simpson, consulting editor; Howard Greenwalt, business manager; (seated) E. Harold Mohn, publisher; James L. Riedy, production manager.

plate 22

Editorial Council of *The Methodist Story* in 1963 is pictured. At center below the window are Edwin H. Maynard, editor, and Elliott L. Fisher, publisher.

Celebrating the tenth anniversary of *The Methodist Story* in 1966 are (left to right) Howard Greenwalt, publisher; Edwin H. Maynard, editor; Carolyn Tah, secretary; and Darrell R. Shamblin, associate editor.

plate 23

Curtis A. Chambers came from a pastorate in Pennsylvania in 1959 to be editor of EUB adult church-school publications. Four years later he joined the staff of *Church and Home* (1966 photo).— *Photo courtesy of United Methodist Archives*

Prime mover in organizing communication activities in the Evangelical United Brethren Church was Paul V. Church, general secretary of the Council of Administration in the 1960s.— *Photo courtesy of Marietta Church*

Artist Edward J. Mikula poses with the Cross and Flame emblem he had designed in 1968.

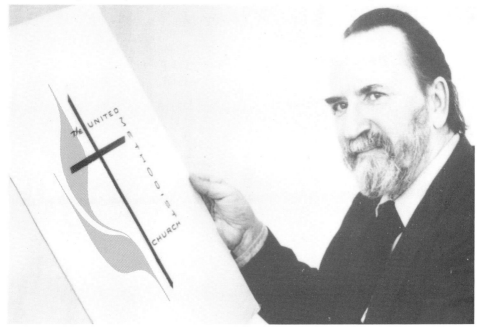

plate 24

After his election as executive secretary of United Methodist Communications in 1973, Curtis A. Chambers established his headquarters office in Dayton, where he is shown.

The news staff about 1974-75 includes (front, left to right) Martha Man, Bruce Mosher, Charlotte O'Neal and (rear) Arthur West, Winston H. Taylor, Robert Lear and Thomas S. McAnally.—*Photo courtesy of Thomas S. McAnally*

Editing film in the old McGavock Street, building in Nashville, are (front to rear) Steve Jackson, Dixie Parman, and Vilmars Zile.

plate 25

Ground was broken for a new building in Nashville in September 1979. The erstwhile hardhats riding the bulldozer are Peggy J. West and Curtis A. Chambers.

Construction continues at 810 Twelfth Avenue, South.

After consecration of the new building March 28, 1981, an open house displayed it to visitors. Curtis A. Chambers (center) greets F. Thomas Trotter (left) of the General Board of Higher Education and Ministry, Mary Lou Spencer and Harry C. Spencer.

plate 26

Hollywood actress Maureen O'Sullivan plays a leading
role in *One Who Was There*, a film built around the
Easter story. She and her daughter, Tisa Farrow, played
Mary Magdalene at different ages.

Donald B. Moyer works at his desk. He was editorial
director in the Evanston office at the time of his violent
death in 1980.

While open house visitors look at the sound lab, a
videographer gets pictures of Vilmars Zile (left front)
and Don Hughes demonstrating the *Connection* radio
show control room.

plate 27

Officers of the General Commission on Communication elected for 1981-84 are (left to right) Charles Cappleman, president; Barbara Blackstone, vice president; and Noah Long, secretary, photographed in Dayton, Ohio, with Wright brothers memorabilia.

Fire fighters work with gutted offices of *The Interpreter* in Dayton after an early morning fire in 1981. Amid the smokey ruins Leonard Perryman writes a news story about the fire.

plate 28

A stageful of talent gives a program of music and testimony to kick off the Television Presence and Ministry campaign on September 20, 1981. Hosting the program is singer Carol Lawrence (in white gown at right), a United Methodist. The show was uplinked from Opryland at Nashville and sent by satellite to groups meeting all across the country.

Carol Lawrence talks with a child during the show.

plate 29

A series of workshops on communication techniques reached Hispanic local churches across the United States and Puerto Rico in the mid-1980s. At a training session for leaders, Wil Bane of UMCom demonstrates a video camera to (left to right) Edith LaFontaine, Roy D. Barton, José Velasquez, Julio Gómez and Ruben Sáenz.

Hispanic communicators are Finees Flores (left), for eleven years editor of El Intérprete and a member of the promotional materials staff, and Roy D. Barton, whose service included presidency of La Junta Consultiva de Comunicaciones and membership on the General Commission on Communication.

plate 30

Jay Voorhees is at the panel in the modern video control room in the Nashville studios.

Howard Clinebell of the School of Theology at Claremont leads in the teaching video, *Growing Through Grief*, in 1984. Present at the taping was UMCom's Suzy Loftis Heydel.

During most of the 1980s the field staff consisted of (left to right) M. Ervin Dailey, Paula C. Watson and W. Cannon Kinnard.

plate 31

The lavish pageant *Festival 200* helped the General Conference celebrate the 1984 American Methodist Bicentennial. UMCom public relations staff worked with the Bicentennial Committee, and William R. Richards was producer.

Peggy W. Welshans, longtime treasurer and chief financial officer for UMCom, makes a presentation.

Officers for the quadrennium 1985-88 are (left to right) Roy D. Barton, vice president; Ruth Daugherty, co-vice president; William K. Quick, secretary; and Bishop Louis W. Schowengerdt, president.

plate 32

InfoServ celebrates its tenth anniversary in 1985. Sam Barefield, director at the time, shows the plaque. Two associate general secretaries related to the project are at far right: Peggy J. West of Production and Distribution and Readus J. Watkins of Program and Benevolence Interpretation.

Among those breaking ground for the 1985-86 enlargement of the Nashville building are (left to right) Wilford V. Bane, Roger L. Burgess, Peggy W. Welshans and Tony Pilversack.

Good neighbors are employees of Rochelle Center, a sheltered workshop for persons with handicapping conditions. They do contract work for UMCom, and as a thank-you they decorated a Christmas tree at the UMCom building.

plate 33

Current and former editorial, circulation, art and administrative staff of *The Interpreter* celebrate the program journal's thirtieth anniversary with a cake in the spring of 1987. Darrell R. Shamblin (seated center) is editor. Others include (seated, left) Laura Okumu, associate editor; (in the second row, left to right) Joretta Purdue, managing editor; Donald E. Collier, associate publisher; and (far right) Roger L. Burgess, publisher. Barbara Dunlap-Berg, editorial consultant, is in the third row, far right.

Members of La Junta Consultiva de Comunicaciones, Hispanic advisory group, for 1989-92, meet with the editor of *El Intérprete*, Edith LaFontaine (front row, center).

plate 34

Laura Okumu (far right), who became editor of *The Interpreter* in 1988, checks a page layout with designer Suzanne Sloan (second from right) as art department director Dani Aguila (left) and managing editor Joretta Purdue review other layouts.

Directors of conference media resource centers are key persons in the network served by EcuFilm. UMCom staff led a United Methodist section of an inter-denominational gathering in Houston in 1980. Diane Cristina (left), EcuFilm manager, and Peggy J. West, associate general secretary of Production and Distribution, are shown.

A constant stream of promotional materials comes from the Division of Program and Benevolence Interpretation. Barbara Dunlap-Berg, editorial director, and Pablo Garzon, assistant editor of *El Intérprete*, look at one of them.

plate 35

Beginning in 1985, a public relations campaign around the theme "Catch the Spirit" uses television spots filmed at a balloon ascension in Texas.

Among the "Catch the Spirit" publicity items were billboards, this one next to an ad for liquor.

plate 36

When UMCom was ready with a television program late in 1985, *Catch the Spirit* became the name of the show. On the set for the program are the first co-hosts: Hilly Hicks and Emily Simer.

Hilly Hicks (center) and the cameraman attract attention during work on a China special for *Catch the Spirit* in 1987.

plate 37

Key figures in *Catch the Spirit* for 1989-90 were (left to right) Kenneth Briggs, commentator; Anisa Mehdi and Hilly Hicks, co-hosts; and Kathleen LaCamera, producer.

With Roger L. Burgess (left), general secretary, are officers of the General Commission on Communication for 1989-92: Mary Silva, vice president; Bishop Rueben P. Job, president; and James W. Lane, secretary.

plate 38

Edgar A. Gossard (far left corner of table, writing) and Susan Peek (right foreground) represent UMCom for a video teleconference group in Nashville. The Howard Clinebell video *Growing Through Grief* was shown simultaneously to groups in Nashville, Seattle, San Antonio and Atlanta. Then participants were on the telephone line with Dr. Clinebell and other groups. Ted McEachern (right front) led the Nashville group.

Planning is an important function for UMCom, involving commission members and staff. This is a small group session at a 1988 retreat for staff.

plate 39

At a 1989 planning session for the Korean program journal, Donald E. Collier, publisher, studies items on newsprint with Eun Chul Cho, pastor of First Korean United Methodist Church in Chicago.

Editor of the new journal, called *United Methodist Family*, is Jungrea H. Chung, shown with Darrell R. Shamblin, associate publisher of the agency's three magazines.

Rows of computers, electric typewriters, and telephones in the news room for the 1988 General Conference in St. Louis testify to the communication revolution when compared with the early press rooms of Methodist Information.

plate 40

The facade of the headquarters building of United Methodist Communications in Nashville features the UMCom logo and the United Methodist Cross and Flame emblem.

Roger L. Burgess, general secretary, works with Betty Van Dyke, administrative assistant to two general secretaries from 1973 to 1989.

Elected staff of UMCom in early 1990 are (seated, left to right) Peggy W. Welshans, treasurer; Roger L. Burgess, general secretary; and Newtonia Harris Coleman; associate general secretary for administration. Standing are the associate general secretaries for the three divisions: Donald E. Collier, Program and Benevolence Interpretation; Peggy J. West, Production and Distribution; and Nelson Price, Public Media.

The million dollars that had been advanced by the General Council on Finance and Administration to pay costs of the failed campaign became $1.3 million when interest was added. A heavy share of the burden to devise a strategy for repayment fell on Welshans as chief financial officer.

Budgets were trimmed in every department and salary raises were deferred. Staff morale was low, but the reduced staff labored on under difficulty. As the payback began, some staff took on extra tasks from the positions that had been eliminated; others found ways to save a few dollars here and a few there in purchasing supplies. Those who traveled looked for air fare bargains and cheap accommodations; some absorbed portions of their travel costs personally.

By heroic effort the debt was retired in three years—a feat many felt impossible. The liberating final payment was made at the end of 1984. Subsequent study by financial analysts showed that the agency emerged leaner, but more efficient and stronger financially.

Public Relations

The years from 1980 to the present saw major developments in public relations for the denomination. That story actually began in 1978 when the CBS 60 *Minutes* broadcast an exposé of supposed abuses at the church-related chain of retirement communities, Pacific Homes. Maynard was assigned to work with major players in behalf of the church: the Division of Health and Welfare in the Board of Global Ministries, the General Council on Finance and Administration, and the Southern California-Arizona Conference. Larry Womack of Nashville was retained as public relations counsel. Efforts were made to counteract innuendos and misinformation. Fact sheets were issued to challenge statements made in the TV show, the *Wall Street Journal* and elsewhere.

Class action lawsuits against the homes and the annual conference were settled out of court. The chain of events illuminated a need for conferences and institutions to clarify their relationships. It also underscored the need for professional activities to provide positive information about the church to national media and to contest false or misleading statements.

It had been clear from the beginning of UMCom that the agency had responsibility for public relations for the denomination as well as for whatever public relations it needed for its own work. What was not clear was how the two functions could be handled without conflict of interest. When Lyndell D. Smith became director of public relations in 1977, her work was defined almost entirely as representing the agency. She edited the newsletter, *UMCommunicator*; prepared annual reports; created displays for meetings; and did some media relations. Smith chaired a staff task force working on ways to differentiate the two functions and develop a strategy for denominational public relations.

During the time he was assigned to public relations, Maynard's efforts were devoted almost entirely to interpreting the church's position in regard to the Pacific Homes lawsuits. He took a few other initiatives, including airport advertising displays at the time of the 1980 General and Jurisdictional Conferences.

William R. Richards in Nashville took over public relations for the denomination in January 1981. Another round of public debate soon began when *60 Minutes* and *Reader's Digest* renewed attacks on the World Council of Churches and National Council of the Churches of Christ in the U.S.A., both having United Methodist support.

Along with media contacts and other activities, Richards introduced a plan to coach bishops and other church leaders for television interviews. He arranged for United Methodist spokespersons to be available for television, radio and newspapers. After Smith's departure in the financial cutbacks of 1982, public relations for UMCom became Richards' responsibility also, with the understanding that it would be handled by other staff under his direction.

In 1984 a public relations campaign was begun on the theme, "The World Is Our Parish." The campaign included packets containing brochures on each United Methodist agency.

It met with modest success, but was soon overshadowed by a new "Catch the Spirit" campaign involving broadcast spots, billboards, newspaper ads and even T-shirts. Then came the TV program, *Catch the Spirit* (Chapter 10).

The campaign theme came from Tennessee Annual Conference, where a 1983 motion asked for development of a public relations campaign to counter negative images of the church resulting from allegations in national magazines and network television. Working with a professional public relations agency, a committee of the conference developed the "Catch the Spirit" theme and, when funded by the 1984 conference, launched the program with billboards, newspaper ads, bumper stickers, radio spot announcements, and other resources. Related to the campaign was the Conference Committee on Communication, chaired by Roger L. Burgess until his appointment as UMCom general secretary. He was succeeded as chair by the Rev. Edward Britt, who had chaired the PR campaign committee.

Richards and others planning churchwide public relations liked the "Catch the Spirit" theme and negotiated with the conference for permission to use it. One by-product was a set of television spot announcements, created as a joint venture between UMCom and Tennessee Conference. Under UMCom auspices, the TV spots, radio spots, billboards and other media soon were seen nationwide. Before long the name was loaned to the forthcoming television program.

In 1989, when Richards moved into media marketing, public relations responsibility was assumed by the general secretary, with assistance by a PR firm. Suzanne Price of the UMCom staff continued as the administrative assistant for PR.

Meanwhile, in 1984, the 200th anniversary of the Christmas Conference of 1784 was celebrated. It was a bicentennial year, with its climax at General Conference in Baltimore. The public relations office was deeply involved, and Richards worked with the United Methodist and Pan-Methodist committees. He was producer for an extravagant pageant at General Conference. UMCom prepared an abundance of bicentennial resources, including printed materials, novelty items and audiovisuals (Chapter 11).

The Burgess Era

Chambers continued as general secretary until the 12-year tenure limit approached. His resignation took effect in the fall of 1984, and the commission selected as the new general secretary Roger L. Burgess.

A "preacher's kid" from northwestern Iowa, Burgess was graduated in 1950 from Morningside, where for two years as a student he directed the college press bureau. He then joined the staff of the National Conference of Methodist Youth in Nashville, where among other duties he edited a devotional guide, *Power*, and a youth newspaper, *Concern*. While an editor there, when chided for some infraction, he claimed protection in the maxim that dictionaries follow usage, declaring: "We *write* the dictionary."

He moved to the Board of Temperance in Washington, D.C., where he edited publications and became director of communications. Next he spent three years in a private design business and with an interfaith service program. In 1968 he returned to church administration as general secretary of the Board of Hospitals and Homes, which in the 1972 restructure carried him into the Board of Global Ministries. In 1974 he joined the United Methodist Publishing House, where he was editorial director for general church periodicals, then vice president for public relations 1976-84.

Along the way he did graduate study at Yale and American Universities and was awarded the LL.D. degree by his alma mater in 1965. He edited the *Daily Christian Advocate* for the General Conferences of 1976, 1980 and 1984 and had articles printed in more than 40 church and secular periodicals.

With the UMCom debt paid off and 1984 General Conference authorization of new funding for telecommunications through regular church channels, the stage was set for new ventures. Burgess turned at once to television. Within months the Nashville studio was producing a well-received weekly program, *Catch the Spirit*. For the agency as a whole, he increased staff salaries and realigned some staff positions. Long-range planning, already in place, was given a new emphasis.

In 1983-84 the perennial question of location had surfaced again. Chambers initiated more studies. It was determined that the Dayton headquarters should give way to Nashville, where the largest number of UMCom employees worked. The change took effect when Dr. Burgess assumed office in October of 1984.

Burgess initiated new studies of the P&BI offices in Evanston and Dayton. Those locations had been predicated on proximity to the General Council on Finance and Administration and the General

Council on Ministries. Combining them in Nashville was proposed to build staff unity, facilitate administration, and save travel and telephone costs. An addition was made to the Nashville building, and a largely new P&BI staff united there in the fall of 1986. The savings were used to strengthen resources for several departments.

The field staff of UMCom had experienced many locations in the administrative structure. Begun in the old Commission on Promotion and Cultivation, it first had the sole task of promoting giving for benevolence funds. In 1973 it was transferred to the short-lived Division of Research, Education and Liaison, where staffers were asked to help also with training in communication skills. Then came the Office of Communication Education and Field Service. Back to P&BI in 1977, they still were expected to represent all of UMCom.

In 1989 something resembling the old REAL Division was created under Shirley Whipple Struchen, formerly of the Public Media Division, as director of conference services. The regionally deployed field staff, one for each jurisdiction, were asked to represent promotion, education and all aspects of UMCom.

New Initiatives

The years from 1972 onward were at first a time for restructure and integrating the work of what had been separate agencies. Increasingly the story becomes one of new initiatives. It was not long before UMCom could be seen as a co-ordinated agency representing the denomination's communication interests in all areas—far more than a continuation of the work of its predecessors.

The overview in Chapter 8 has told of the organization, its people, and some of the innovations. Other ways UMCom applied the fast-developing communication technologies are recounted in Chapter 10. Subsequent chapters detail the agency's work in the broadcast media, film and video production, and publication—as well as other dimensions.

The complexity of the story attests to the wisdom of the General Conference of 1972 when it set up one communication agency to deal with myriad opportunities opened by the communication revolution.

·9·

Still the Revolution

The phrase "communication revolution" entered the language gradually. By the early 1960s no one could fail to be aware of the flood of developments in technology—each advance opening the way for dozens more.

In December 1964 Harry Spencer and TRAFCO brought some two hundred Methodists from all over the United States to New York for a four-day consultation on "The Church in the Communications Revolution." The idea of "revolution" appeared more and more in what church communication leaders said and wrote.

And they strained energies and budgets to keep up with the revolution.

Considering the high costs of new technologies and the risks in using them, United Methodists established a creditable record. Often they were pioneers.

The ground-breaking call-in radio show of the late '60s, *Night Call* (Chapter 5), is an example. Circuitry for that program, invented by Warren Braun and patented by TRAFCO, opened new options for radio. But high costs drove the program off the air at a time when it was carrying on a much-needed national dialog.

90

Video Takes Over

In 1972 the Rev. Earl Kenneth Wood of the Division of Program and Benevolence Interpretation went to a commercial producer (over protests of the Division of Production and Distribution) to shoot a movie by video—and then transfer the result to film. Today Production and Distribution does more shooting and editing by video than film. The end product may be either—or both.

From the user's standpoint, the tide is running strong toward the video cassette. One annual conference reported in 1989 that two thirds of the rentals from its resource center were video. Furman York, director of EcuFilm, reported a 50 percent increase in rental and sales of video in 1988.

The reason is the video cassette recorder, usually referred to as VCR. The VCR makes it easier than ever to show pictures. VCRs are popular in homes to record and replay television programs or show rented or purchased movies. At church the video player and a television set make it easy to show movies—or still pictures in what had been the filmstrip format. Church school teachers—and others who present programs to groups—find the VCR a welcome liberation from projectors and screens. Many churches purchase video cassettes for their own resource centers. They could not afford several hundred dollars for a 16mm film, but they can buy a videotape for under thirty dollars.

In a very real way video has fulfilled TRAFCO dreams from thirty years earlier, when there was a search for a convenient and inexpensive way to project pictures. For a time TRAFCO tested a variety of Super-8 systems that offered simplified, cartridge-loaded projectors. The Commission on Promotion and Cultivation marketed Super-8 projectors and supported the system by transferring its own films from 16mm to 8mm (Super-8) and urging other agencies to do so. It turned out that Super 8 was not the answer, but at the beginning of the 1990s video is accomplishing what earlier efforts failed to do.

Video cassette recorders, in only 1 percent of American households in 1980 zoomed to estimates of 60 percent to 70 percent in 1989, and the forecast for 1995 is 85 percent. The popularity of video, Peggy West points out, opens the way for the church's audiovisuals to be used in homes as well as churches. Many of the UMCom videos, such as the *Questions of Faith* series, lend themselves to home use, she says.

Video has been used in many ways besides as a format for audiovisuals. In 1985 for the first time members of the General Commission on Communication witnessed a video annual report in place of the customary paper booklet. UMCom helped the planning committee for General Conference arrange for giant screens to show speakers at St. Louis in 1988 and UMCom provided the staff to run the video cameras.

Some local churches have found it beneficial to produce their own videotapes—especially since development of the highly portable camcorder. UMCom has provided ideas and advice to congregations through manuals and columns in *The Interpreter*, both for locally produced video and for making use of videotapes purchased or rented. Help has been given to annual conferences to train their people in use of videos, often with UMCom field staff giving the training. The result: hundreds of churches are finding video a useful tool for financial campaigns, membership training, youth fellowship adventures, Sunday school classes and dozens of other applications.

The Toll-Free Number

Innovative ideas for UMCom have come from staff, commission members, consultants or rank-and-file United Methodists. Faced with many options, staff have revamped budgets and made painful choices. The result has been new ways for the church to communicate. Video is one; another is InfoServ.

InfoServ put to church use technical advances in the telephone system: the toll-free WATS line, switching equipment and improved clarity of long-distance calls. Field staff reported a need for a way to give church members quick, cost-free answers to questions on benevolences, programs and resources and to counteract misleading rumors. UMCom assigned people to match the need with technology and the result was an information system that has been copied by several denominations and envied by more.

By dialing InfoServ's toll-free "800" number, the caller gets a live person on the telephone line. This person is prepared to answer questions, receive comment or complaint, and look up information. Phones are answered by InfoServ's "consultants," who have instant access to millions of bits of information in carefully organized files.

Preliminary work on the concept was done by Sue Couch, UMCom director of public relations, and the Rev. James C. Campbell, head of the Division of Production and Distribution. Development and design (and then management) were by the Rev. Samuel S. Barefield of his staff and Peggy West as assistant director. After two years of planning, InfoServ went on-line October 1, 1974, and logged 50 calls its first day.

By 1980 it averaged 112 calls a day and in 1988, 140 not counting taped messages. The biggest year ever was 1988, in which 33,859 questions were answered. General Conference brought 1,640 direct calls, and 5,237 callers listened to daily taped summaries. During jurisdictional conferences, when bishops were being elected, July 14 was the all-time peak day with 1,961 calls.

Calls are handled by a staff of three full-time and six part-time consultants. Most of the work is accomplished with two WATS lines, although extras are added for General and Jurisdictional Conferences. A new line with its own number was added in 1989 to deal with the high volume of requests for addresses of churches. It costs UMCom about sixty-seven cents to answer the average InfoServ inquiry.

The telephone industry solved most of the phone problems but it was up to UMCom to learn how to gather the right information and have it at the fingertips of those who answered the phone. West used her library experience to get that started. General agencies of the church agreed to assign staff as liaison to InfoServ. Sometimes callers were referred to them, but InfoServ tried to give the answer themselves while on-line or with a fast call-back.

Information files were maintained manually from the start. Computerization seemed inevitable, and by 1987 computers were helping keep some records up to date, but the main system continued to be manual—and personal.

Barefield directed InfoServ until 1985, when Woodley McEachern, who had been a telephone consultant almost from the beginning, became director. Because it was interpreting the church to United Methodists, administration was first assigned to the Division of Program and Benevolence Interpretation, soon to the REAL division, then back to P&BI, then to Production and Distribution, and finally to P&BI again.

When church members and clergy use InfoServ, some calls seem funny and others are dead serious, but each question is important to the caller and is treated with respect. Some sample questions: "What time does the sun come up on Easter?" "I need a speaker on family life or stress management—either one will do." "Are there any garbage bags with the logo, 'The World Is Our Parish'?" "What is the address of the new episcopal area in South Georgia?" "What is the Advance project number for flood relief to Bangladesh?" "How can I get a loan to attend college?" "What is the date for Native Awareness Sunday?" "How can we get a charter for our United Methodist Men?" And so on.

More calls come from pastors than lay persons. The most frequent topics are some aspect of church program or benevolences. Surveys show that most callers are pleased with the speed and quality of response. More than 70 percent of callers are local church folks and the heart of InfoServ is interaction between caller and consultant.

For eight years InfoServ at night put on an automatic answering machine a brief tape recording, "Newsline Global," a message from the Board of Global Ministries, changed weekly. An increase in line charges made the service too costly to continue in 1982.

Beginning in 1976, during each General Conference daily summaries of news from the conference are played twenty-four hours a day in addition to human answers to specific questions. In 1980 the recorded summary was played 16,000 times and 3,500 callers talked with consultants. Beginning in 1976 a Spanish InfoServ line has been open during General Conference, and in 1988 a Korean tape was added. Recorded summaries during Jurisdictional Conferences provide episcopal ballot results.

94

On-Line With Computers

Computers during the 1970s were costly, room-filling affairs, suitable for the Board of Pensions but not UMCom. When the general secretary's office purchased word processing equipment, the divisions soon clamored for computers. A heated debate over the merits of mainframe computers versus stand-alone units ensued and a staff task force was appointed to plan a strategy for computerizing the agency.

Priority was given to mailing list management in the Division of Production and Distribution in Nashville. Susan Peek in Central Addressing in 1978 acquired a computer in the Basic Four system promoted by the General Council on Finance and Administration as a standard. That computer could handle the 300,000 subscribers to *The Interpreter* as well as lists for News Service, the agency newsletter and other mailings.

As computers became smaller year by year, the desktop unit, or personal computer, opened new possibilities. Soon computers appeared in other UMCom offices, and staff began communicating with each other by electronic mail in a system set up by Peek, using as a base NewsNet, a "common carrier" accessed by long distance telephone.

News Service in 1977 set up a central news desk to replace separate mailings from its five offices. Copy was received from the news writers and edited in New York, then sent by the mag-card system over phone lines to Nashville, where it was duplicated and mailed. By 1982 the central news desk was in Nashville, so mag-card transmission was out.

For communication among its scattered offices News Service installed Telautograph Omnifax machines in 1977. Six years later they were replaced by 3M models that could transmit a page in forty seconds. The next step in 1984 was computers, enabling staff to send stories by phone from New York or Washington, or wherever they might be on assignment, at 420 words a minute. Small, portable Radio Shack units were purchased for each newswriter.

The 1983 World Council of Churches Assembly in Vancouver, Canada, was the first event from which, as a test, United Methodist

News Service transmitted its news coverage by computer. The next year copy was sent from General Conference in Baltimore to the Nashville office by computer, via NewsNet. The news stories could be seen on NewsNet by the computer-wise public.

Soon all news releases were being stored in the data bank at NewsNet. Current stories could be viewed or printed out by anyone who had a computer and a modem to connect it to phone lines. Topics could be researched in back years by giving the computer key words to look for.

In a Computer-Based Communications Task Force, ordered by the 1980 General Conference, UMCom and the General Council on Ministries worked four years on strategies for computer use in the church. In September 1983 the task force sponsored a consultation and demonstration attended by representatives of seven general agencies, two annual conferences, and three local churches. The electronic newsletter, *United Methodist Information*, already tested for four months, was demonstrated to participants.

Also in 1983, Peek led in development of the CBC network, which fed into the CircuitWriter Network, by 1989 linking some 130 computer users who shared ideas and resources via electronic mail and a computer bulletin board. UMCom supported mutual help among computer users and cooperated with the Church Computer User's Network. The newsletter *United Methodist Information* was continued on the electronic network.

An early success for CBC '84 came at the General and Jurisdictional Conferences of 1984, when for the first time modem-owning computer users anywhere could get current information about what was happening. From the site of the General Conference in Baltimore, CBC '84 carried an electronic newsletter each day including all news reports of United Methodist News Service, the text of InfoServ's daily reports, commentary by Elliott Wright of Religious News Service, occasional transcripts from the *Daily Christian Advocate*, and bulletins updated three times a day. From the five jurisdictional conferences, which met simultaneously, volunteers helped provide running accounts of balloting for bishops, episcopal assignments, and other news. A similar service was provided in 1988 by CircuitWriter.

UMCom has been involved in training for use of computers for communication and has encouraged annual conference communication units to offer such training. Some of this was done in cooperation with the United Methodist Publishing House, which had become a vendor of computer equipment and programs.

Since 1985 a computerized sales and rental system keeps track of users of more than eight hundred audiovisual titles for EcuFilm.

Other UMCom units use computers for management chores, word processing, and typesetting (electronic publishing). Printed publications, especially in the Division of Program and Benevolence Interpretation, have been put out with greater efficiency, thanks to computers. Computers are particularly useful to the magazines.

Early in 1989 *The Interpreter* went on-line with a system by which writers and editors prepare copy on computer terminals and the copy was transmitted by modem to typesetting machines at the United Methodist Publishing House. Then with the closing of UMPH's Parthenon Press at the end of 1989, the magazine went to a desktop-publishing prepress operation connected with a commercial magazine printing company.

Facsimile, commonly known as fax, developed parallel with computer-based communication. In fact, the fax machine so popular in offices today also depends on sophisticated electronics.

The speedy, user-friendly fax of today had primitive ancestors, and communication offices were among the first to use them. In the 1950s the Commission on Promotion and Cultivation in Chicago installed a Thermofax machine, which used a heat process. It was slow and smelly, but it could send a written message over the telephone line and print hard copy at the other end. It required special heat-sensitive paper, which had to be unloaded and reloaded on a rotating drum for each page, and transmission required up to five minutes per page—a cause for secretarial groans when word came that a 20-page document was coming in from New York, starting at a quarter past four.

The Promotion and Cultivation office used fax to exchange documents related to its promotional work with the Board of Missions in New York. Before long one of the agencies in Nashville acquired Thermofax. As soon as the instrument's capabilities became known, it was borrowed by others—among them the regional directors of Methodist Information.

By 1990 every United Methodist general agency (with one or two possible exceptions) was using fax and many annual conferences had installed fax.

Teleconferencing

Another dimension of telephone communication is teleconferencing. The technological key to this is called a bridge. The device permits callers on several different lines to talk and listen to one another. Early versions were limited in the number of lines that could be connected and voices often were faint. Improvements were made on both points.

As early as the 1960s Gene Carter was using telephone for long-distance committee meetings and urging others to try it. Acceptance was slow because of value attached to face-to-face contact, but rising travel costs stimulated meetings by telephone.

Increasingly, UMCom staff used conference calls for meetings of three or more persons in different cities. Committee meetings of an hour or longer were held by teleconference, enhanced by speaker phones that permitted several participants at each location. Entire committees met by conference telephone: the Executive Staff of UMCom (especially during the financial crunch of 1982), the Executive Committee of the General Commission on Communication, and the Steering Committee of the Television Presence and Ministry. A crucial meeting of the Steering Committee tied in fifty locations.

UMCom encouraged other church agencies to hold down travel by telephone meetings. Training was offered and guidelines recommended. UMCom became a broker of teleconference services when in 1982 it contracted with International Telecom Systems to purchase bridging services for the denomination. UMCom bought the services wholesale and sold them to church agencies at lower than commercial rates. More recently the contract has been with the Public Service Satellite Consortium.

Today the state of the art permits an unlimited number of parties anywhere in the United States—or even overseas—to be connected by telephone.

Television teleconferencing is also possible, but high cost limits church use. A joint venture with the United Methodist Association of Communicators (UMAC), initiated by its president, the Rev. Robert L. Robertson of Texas, was a closed circuit video hook-up that enabled UMAC to hold its 1974 annual meeting at six locations, greatly reducing members' travel.

Bouncing Off the Satellite

Satellite communication is generally used for video teleconferencing. Electronic signals are sent into space to a transponder on a satellite high above the earth. The signals can be received by dish antennas anywhere within the "footprint" of the satellite.

This was the latest technology, used in 1981 for the launch of the Television Presence and Ministry campaign. The program was presented before a live audience in Nashville and uplinked to the satellite. At the same moment groups were gathered at 144 locations, many of them in Holiday Inns. Participants at each location could see and hear the program on television monitors. An estimated six thousand persons viewed the event.

Television communication by satellite can be interactive so that, as in the telephone conference call, participants can speak to and listen to one another. And they can see and be seen. In 1990 the most promising use is for training sessions in which a lecturer, or panel at one or more locations, present information seen and heard by clusters gathered in a number of other locations. Often this is a collaboration by UMCom, education specialists and the United Methodist Publishing House. The latter does programming over its Cokesbury Satellite Television Network and has offered one downlink antenna free to each annual conference. Some institutions, such as universities and seminaries, have set up rooms equipped for such sessions and offer them for hire.

Video and teleconferencing were combined in 1984 in a training event for pastors on grief counseling. Arranged by Peggy West in collaboration with the School of Theology at Claremont (California), it featured Howard Clinebell of the Claremont faculty, whose work with members of a grief support group was shown by video to enrolled participants at four locations on two days. Twice each day all locations were linked by telephone for discussion with Dr. Clinebell.

The next year UMCom helped the Western Jurisdiction arrange a series of four continuing education sessions for pastors linking eleven locations. After a videotape presentation and local discussion, all locations were joined for conversation with each other and professors at two seminaries. Two of the discussion sessions were by conference video and two by audio only.

Another use of satellites is to send programs to television stations. At the 1980 General Conference UMCom used satellites to send cable TV systems two hour-long news summaries of the conference. The service was repeated in 1984 and 1988. For viewers of the Cokesbury Satellite Television Network there were 15-minute daily news summaries.

Catch the Spirit programs ride to the satellite and back as cable systems transmit them to local cable companies.

An international satellite feed was arranged in 1979 for the Women's Division of the Board of Global Ministries. It linked Geneva, Switzerland, with Lincoln, Nebraska, so four executives of the World Council of Churches could talk for an hour with women attending a national seminar in Lincoln. Producers were John Rider, a member of UMCom's commission, and staffer Bruce Mosher.

The Cable Option

Cable networks, which are the primary carriers of UMCom's television show, *Catch the Spirit*, in 1990 serve more than half of all U.S. homes. It is a matter of debate whether the number will continue to grow, or if use of private dish antennas (shrinking yearly in physical size) will render cable systems obsolete. In 1990 the convenience of cable (no aiming of an antenna) and its reliably clear picture seem to ensure its future. But two million Americans own satellite dishes.

While UMCom had scored many successes in placing programs on TV networks and over-the-air stations, the most reliable and least costly placement has been on cable. For *Catch the Spirit* annual conferences and local churches have had better success with cable, mainly because of the high cost of buying time for over-the-air broadcast. Some churches have used the cost-free community access channel that most cable systems provide.

Interactive television, some of whose applications were described in Chapter 1, depend on cable. Those wires may be the essential link for the "electronic cottage" of the future.

Some special services by UMCom depend on cable. At St. Louis in 1988 General Conference delegates could tune to channel 8 or 12 in their hotel rooms each morning and see a summary of the previous day's actions, prepared by UMCom staff and transmitted to the hotels by closed circuit. A similar system was used in 1973 in Louisville, Kentucky, when UMCom's Mosher collaborated with Board of Global Ministries communication staff to provide morning devotions, videotaped on the spot and delivered by cable to the hotels. In the years since similar applications have been made for other United Methodist meetings.

Technology does not stand still. No one can predict what it will be in another fifty years—or even another decade. But if the record of the past is a guide, United Methodist Communications will be monitoring each new development in the continuing communication revolution and looking for ways improvements in technology can help the church tell its story.

·10·

Getting on the Tube

United Methodists want their church to be seen on television's magic tube. They view TV as an instrument of evangelizing and creating public awareness.

Or pride: "When I turn on my TV, I want to see the Cross and Flame."

Church efforts to use effectively the medium for the Christian message go back to the early days of TV. The creative work of TRAFCO in the 1950s was a start. The intervening years brought the television evangelists, who raised millions of dollars on the air, who purchased broadcast time, and who eventually owned TV stations and elaborate studios. At the same time networks and individual stations gave less and less time for free "public service" broadcasts—a trend later hastened by deregulation.

Effective use of television calls for creative program ideas, competent people to produce the programs—and money. UMCom, and TRAFCO before it, have scored very well with the first two. The nagging problem has been money.

In TRAFCO days, permission was received at various times for special funding to be solicited beyond the basic budget of World Service money. There were some successes, particularly with the Children's Television Fund, begun as a memorial to three staff members. Then as now it seemed that the typical United Methodist was eager to see his church on the tube but loath to give extra money to make it happen.

102

During the first UMCom quadrennium, 1973-76, acclaim and awards were given to spot announcements offered to stations for use during children's programs. The 30-second spots aimed to build positive values among child viewers with simple minidramas demonstrating such virtues as taking turns and helping each other. They were produced jointly with other denominations and continued in use for more than a decade. Also for children were three 12-minute films for use on cable television and in churches and schools: the *Magic Circle Conflict Curriculum*.

Six hour-long programs on family values were produced as a series. They were *Six American Families*, produced by Group W (Westinghouse), in co-operation with UMCom and the United Church of Christ Office of Communication. The arrangement between the broadcaster and the two church units helped placement of the programs. The series was supported by a book.

A series on interpersonal relationships, *Learning to Live*, was released for broadcast and cable television and as an audiovisual resource. *Learning to Live* became one of UMCom's most successful audiovisual ventures, selling many copies through Mass Media Ministries (MMM). (The latter was a private organization based on the East Coast and a pioneer in film distribution to churches and other non-profit groups. MMM had distribution rights to many UMCom productions, often giving them substantial sales and rentals. One of the partners in Mass Media Ministries was Furman York, who in 1984 joined the UMCom staff as director of EcuFilm.)

Also produced in these years was a short film that has had enduring broadcast use and a second career as an audiovisual program (film or video). It is *A Fuzzy Tale*, promoting loving, caring relationships by showing appreciation—the "warm fuzzies." Nelson Price was executive producer and Jeff Weber producer.

Looking for Money

These also were the years of the UMCom study that led to the proposal for a Comprehensive Communication System—a strategy for church use of all the media (Chapter 7). The system recommended major use of print for internal communications at the local church, annual conference and general church levels. For communicating with the general public it proposed using television and radio.

The proposal carried a price tag of $2.3 million a year, of which $500,000 was for the broadcast media. Some of the total could be met from the UMCom budget, but $1.2 million a year of new money was needed.

The proposal went from UMCom to the General Council on Ministries, where it was returned to the communicators to refine, narrow the options, and reduce the cost. This done, it was carried to the General Conference by GCOM, scaled down to $659,000, of which $340,000 was for radio and TV.

As a financial proposal it needed to be submitted in advance to the General Council on Finance and Administration. There it was denied. At Portland, Oregon, members of the 1976 General Conference gave enthusiastic support to the Comprehensive Communication System. Faced with the money factor, they voted by a much lesser margin to request the finance agency to find $659,000 a year. Again GCFA ruled no additional money for communications beyond the regular funding through World Service.

Gloomy UMCom strategists thought all was lost, but then a delegate hitherto unknown to them took the floor. He was Robert D. Cheyne of Arkansas, a layman active in his own church and conference and partner in a successful advertising agency. In a legislative committee he got a new fund plan proposed and on the conference floor he argued: "Believe me, without mass communication you will not achieve your program, . . . you will not tell the United Methodist and Christian program to the world around you." The plan was for a Mass Communications Fund, apportioned at $600,000 a year.

In rare drama on the floor of the General Conference, the house voted three times on the motion. Asking for a show of hands, Bishop Charles F. Golden, who was presiding, announced that the obviously close vote had gone against the fund. After shouted protests, he asked for a second show of hands and then ruled that it had carried. There was a call for a count vote and the third vote authorized the MasCom Fund, 557-367.

Later that year Cheyne was made a member of UMCom's governing committee and gave leadership throughout his allowed eight years.

The MasCom Fund was promoted by UMCom's Division of Program and Benevolence Interpretation. Since it was an apportioned fund, each church was asked to give a specified amount. The MasCom Fund yielded approximately 85 percent of its goal. Over four years it produced a little more than two million dollars that otherwise would not have been available for mass communications. The money was to go mainly for broadcast, but some of it was marked for placing United Methodist stories and spokespersons in all media, for aiding local church newsletter editors, and for expanding InfoServ.

The funds were substantial, yet not enough for a major impact on television. So radio was selected for the first venture. A magazine-format radio program, *Connection*, was created. Major content consisted of interviews with persons about their faith— how the Christian faith had helped them weather a crisis or enabled them to serve others. *Connection* also included devotional moments, music and occasional comment. It was produced by William R. (Bill) Richards, assisted by Samuel Murillo, who began with UMCom as an intern, was invited to join the staff and eventually became producer of *Connection*.

The half-hour program began in October 1977 and at its peak was carried by some 500 radio stations. Annual conferences and even local churches were active in placement. In some cases time was purchased, but two-thirds of the stations aired *Connection* on public service time. It was one of the first radio programs to be distributed by satellite.

Thirty radio spots were produced as part of a multimedia program to support churches' single adult ministries, using the theme "One with Another," introduced in 1979.

Television was not abandoned. During 1977-80 the major UMCom TV production was the series, *Begin With Goodbye*. It explored separations such as moving, divorce, children leaving home, and death. The host was the well-known actor, Eli Wallach. The six programs required more than two years of research, writing and shooting on location. The shows were completed on videotape in the studios of KERA, Dallas, in cooperation with the Southern Educational Communications Association. *Begin With Goodbye* was broadcast by 85 percent of the stations in the Public Broadcasting System and segments were transferred to 16mm film and released as a series for church showings and use by study groups.

TV Presence and Ministry

Nineteen seventy-eight was the year when Charles Cappleman made his electrifying proposal for The United Methodist Church to own a television station. As its president, he addressed the Joint Committee on Communications in New York in October. "Television seems to have become the main enculturing tool of our society," he said, "rather than the home, the church or the school. And this is where the church is missing the boat. Mainline Protestant influence in the television community is almost invisible; the Protestant presence just isn't there."

He urged the church to "seriously investigate the ownership of radio and television stations because, properly managed, they are profitable." Profits, he added, could be plowed back into programming. It was an approach used successfully by the Mormons (Church of Jesus Christ of Latter Day Saints).

The Joint Committee did not immediately endorse the idea, but enthusiastically voted to look into the prospects. A task force was formed and in succeeding months it developed a plan that was submitted to the 1980 General Conference in Indianapolis. It was called Television Presence and Ministry.

The thought that the church might actually own and operate a television station was debated widely. Church periodicals carried editorials and letters to the editor. There were heated discussions in annual conferences, in theological seminaries, and in the Joint Committee on Communications itself.

The committee in November 1979 approved a proposal to the

106

1980 General Conference. There would be a semi-autonomous foundation, controlled by trustees appointed by and accountable to UMCom. The foundation would purchase a station in a medium-sized market, preferably in a region where United Methodists were numerous. Another board, appointed by the foundation, would manage the station, hire staff and supervise the operation. The entire scheme, including the station and production of prime-time programming, would depend upon the raising of $25 million to set up the foundation.

The issue was hotly debated at General Conference. Supporters saw the plan, as Cappleman did, as a chance for the church to earn money for television and have a facility for producing shows that could be used elsewhere. The opposition was concerned about the quality of programming a commercial station with network affiliation would put on the air and also about objectionable commercials, especially advertising beer. There was an amendment requiring the station to operate within terms of the United Methodist Social Creed. In the end the conference voted for the plan by a sizeable majority. A three-year fund-raising campaign would begin January 1, 1981.

One detail that made it easier for delegates to vote for the plan proved also to be a fatal flaw. The money was not to be part of the apportionment system. It was to be raised from United Methodist sources, but outside normal benevolence channels. It was easy for a delegate to think he or she was voting for money someone else would give.

After General Conference what was now named General Commission on Communication, with Cappleman reelected president, established a steering committee to direct the campaign for the $25 million. Fund-raising counsel was retained and a staff hired, headed by A. LeRoy Lightner, an active United Methodist layman with advertising agency experience and once a member of the Commission on Public Relations and Methodist Information. Six regional directors were hired.

Plans were made for the kick-off, an extravagant musical show at the Grand Ole Opry House in Nashville, sent around the country by satellite (Chapter 9). The show was hosted by Carol Lawrence, a

107

popular singer and a United Methodist, and featured an array of musical talent that included another United Methodist local church member, Sarah Cannon, a popular humorist under the stage name of Minnie Pearl. The program included testimony, choral music and an explanation of the campaign with appropriate endorsements. Those who saw it in Nashville and at satellite downlinks around the country gave it good reviews.

Within the steering committee there were divisions of opinion as to how best to implement the plan. General Conference action had authorized station ownership, but all agreed the desired goal was a "United Methodist presence" in television. The station would be a means to that end. Just a few days before the kick-off the Steering Committee pulled back from station ownership and resolved that the $25 million would be used instead as an investment, perhaps in broadcast properties, with the proceeds used to provide United Methodist television programming.

Confusion resulted from the last-minute switch of signals. Some prospective donors were wary of contributing to an investment fund. Despite the resounding endorsement by General Conference, the fact that the Television Presence and Ministry was not included in the ongoing denominational benevolences made it appear somehow to be in competition with the "regular" benevolences. Whatever the reasons, the campaign did not succeed. Giving did not even cover expenses, so when the campaign was shut down, UMCom was left with a million-dollar debt. Many persons who had pledged discontinued payments.

Connection was an early casualty of the agency's retrenchment, but other radio work continued: *The Word—And Music* and co-operative programming such as the United Methodist Series in *The Protestant Hour* and radio programs through the National Council of Churches.

The Protestant Hour was broadcast weekly over as many as 550 radio stations. In 1984 UMCom placed the first-ever woman preacher on the program. She was the Rev. Carol Matteson Cox of New York, preaching the Bicentennial series. A 1989 series by the Rev. William K. Quick of Detroit, two-term commission member and vice president 1985-88, brought an increase in the number of stations carrying the program, which had been in decline. Forty-nine stations were added to the network for his series, and there were 3,600 requests for the book of his sermons.

In television, UMCom continued to place *Six American Families* and *Begin With Goodbye*. There were a few small-scale new productions. United Methodist programming was uplinked weekly for cable systems.

A New Path to Television

After failure of the Television Presence and Ministry, a new study committee was set up to explore future options. The committee used a national questionnaire, held numerous consultations, and cosponsored a theologically oriented conference on "Media Ancient and Modern." The research showed a major concern to help conferences and churches use cable television and video. Planning by the committee led to a television/telecommunication proposal.

Mindful of the Comprehensive Communication System, the committee included other media that rely on electronic technology—for example, computers. It remembered also the comprehensive system's multilevel approach. Whereas the Television Presence and Ministry centered on national programming to be distributed locally, the new proposal stressed operation at local and conference levels along with the national. In fact the financial plan, Television/Telecommunication Fund, apportioned within the World Service Fund, provided that half the money given in each conference should be returned to the conference to pay for its own telecommunication work.

The Bicentennial General Conference in Baltimore in 1984 supported the idea. The Television/Telecommunication Fund was voted as a part of the denomination's regular funding. Television and telecommunications would have some $3.9 million over four years, half of it to be used by UMCom.

By the end of 1984 the campaign debt had been paid off and in 1985 TV/T money began to come in. Things were looking up.

Catch the Spirit

While portions of UMCom's new money went to other areas, such as computer-based communications and teleconferencing, the bulk of it was assigned to television. The decision was to produce a half-hour United Methodist program to be distributed nationally, primarily to cable systems.

The show was *Catch the Spirit*, centerpiece of UMCom programming for the years following its launch in January 1986.

The show's title, borrowed from the public relations campaign, was chosen before UMCom's involvement with Tennessee Annual Conference (Chapter 8). During planning for the program, the Rev. Bruno L. Caliandro of New York, who had been designated as producer, was en route to Nashville to consult with UMCom's Bill Richards. They had been searching for a title. On the way into town from the airport, Caliandro saw one of the "Catch the Spirit" billboards. Richards also had just seen one of the billboards, his first knowledge of the conference campaign. When the two met, each exclaimed that he had the ideal title for the show. At once it was evident that they both wanted "Catch the Spirit." After arrangements were made with the conference, that became the name.

The program's magazine format enabled Caliandro to show United Methodist churches and individuals in acts of service and telling their faith stories. There was room also for some commentary. The Rev. Hilly Hicks and Emily Simer were hosts. Regular commentators were Kathleen LaCamera on films and the Rev. Kenneth Briggs, for many years editor of religion news for the New York *Times*, on the religious scene. Production was in the UMCom studios and on location. Hicks was a regular UMCom staff member and producer in addition to being a host. Simer worked under contract.

The new program was available to any cable television system and, for that matter, to any household with a satellite dish. Initially it was distributed through four cable networks: Christian Broadcast Network, ACTS (Southern Baptist), Black Entertainment Network and Alternate View Network (Shreveport, Louisiana).

110

Annual conferences were urged to take the lead in getting local cable franchise-holders to carry *Catch the Spirit*. The Rev. Keith A. Muhleman was brought from Wisconsin to administer TV/T with an emphasis on working with conferences.

During its first quadrennium there were eighty half-hour *Catch the Spirit* programs, allowing for year-round programming with reruns. The programs told more than 400 stories. Eventually the series was carried on seven national cable networks plus the Armed Forces Radio and Television Service. The cable networks reached 46 million households in 7,000 communities. *Catch the Spirit* also was shown on seventy-five local broadcast and cable stations.

Supplementing the usual content of brief faith stories, several specials were produced. Notable was a report on the church in China, created by a staff team that traveled there in the fall of 1987. It was broadcast December 12 of that year and, like other *Catch the Spirit* programs, was made available as a video for in-church use. The China special was made possible by money from the General Board of Global Ministries, the Park Avenue (New York) United Methodist Church Trust Fund, the American Bible Society and the Seminary Foundation.

As a TV show, *Catch the Spirit* attracted positive comment: "Seeing the program makes me want to work harder in my local church." "I get a lot of energy, recharging my own spirit." "I'm glad our church has this tool for communication." As videotapes, program segments have been used by church school classes and other study groups.

The "Catch the Spirit" public relations campaign (Chapter 9) continued with billboards, newspaper advertisements and other media applications. While representing the church as a whole, the public relations efforts now also supported the TV series to which it had lent its name.

When the 1988 General Conference came, UMCom could report that the TV/T Fund had given the church a regular presence in television and enabled it to move into other electronic media.

Funding for TV/T was continued, but with changes. It would no longer be a separate item, but folded into the World Service money allotted to UMCom. And return of half the money to conferences was discontinued. Henceforth conferences would have to find their own ways to fund telecommunications.

In the new quadrennium, leading into UMCom's fiftieth anniversary year, *Catch the Spirit* was continued, with Anisa Mehdi replacing Simer as co-host while Hicks continued. Caliandro continued as producer, with Kathleen LaCamera as associate producer. In 1989 she was appointed senior producer, and Caliandro became director of program development for the Public Media Division.

Illustrative of program content are these vignettes: a prison ministry by lay volunteers; a United Methodist businessman telling how his firm offers literacy training to employees and customers; the Four Corners Native American Ministry; a wheelchair-bound pastor ministering to handicapped employees of a local Goodwill Industries. And there was another program on China. "Questions of Faith" and "Moment of Faith" features presented a variety of clergy discussing such topics as suffering, Jesus' revolutionary love, and "Who Is My Neighbor?"

More than two dozen "field producers" in various parts of the United States contributed story ideas and, by assignment, produced segments on location.

By the summer of 1989 *Catch the Spirit* was being distributed through six satellite networks and the Armed Forces Radio and Television Service. In addition, more than thirty local broadcast stations and cable systems carried it. Total distribution reached ninety-two of the top hundred TV markets.

Other Programming

In 1988 UMCom joined with twenty-one other denominations and faith groups to form VISN (Vision Interfaith Satellite Network), a consortium mostly of mainline denominations to provide all-day religious programming to cable systems as an alternative to the highly commercialized television evangelists. VISN regularly carries *Catch the Spirit*, *Faces on Faith* and worship services from United Methodist churches. Within a year VISN was being seen in 1,100 communities with four million potential viewers.

Numerous other United Methodist-related programs were seen on VISN. Among them were *Perspectives* with the Rev. Maxie Dunnam, *VISN This Week* with Briggs, *VISN on Film* with LaCamera and the Rev. Robert E. A. Lee, and *Life Lifters* with the Rev. Robert M. (Bob) Holmes.

The cable industry supported VISN as a religious channel and many persons in the industry welcomed it as an alternative to the highly commercialized televangelists. For the churches VISN represented an affordable path to a TV presence.

Serving briefly as first general manager of VISN was a United Methodist, David Ochoa. With his departure in 1988, Wilford V. Bane of the UMCom staff was asked to serve as interim general manager. Bane had been involved, with Price and Caliandro, in the development of VISN and had become a key figure in continuing negotiations for support from the cable industry and in getting denominational leaders to work together. Early in 1990 Bane returned full time to his post as director of media production in UMCom's Division of Production and Distribution.

Named president and chief executive officer for VISN, beginning in March 1990, was Nelson Price. Dr. Price's thirty years with TRAFCO and UMCom—fifteen of them as associate general secretary for the Public Media Division—had been marked by a deep commitment to an ecumenical approach to broadcasting. His appointment neatly blended his concerns for the broadcast media, communication by United Methodists and an ecumenical witness.

During all of these events UMCom continued to work with the Communication Commission of the National Council of Churches. It made a place on television for United Methodist concerns, portrayed through the church's ministries. United Methodist local churches often were featured on special occasions, such as Christmas and Easter. For the 1984 bicentennial of the 1784 Christmas Conference there was a New Year's Eve broadcast from Lovely Lane Chapel in Baltimore and later in the year network broadcast of a special on the history of women in the church.

113

News of religion was provided to 1,250 radio stations through Ecumedia News Service, sponsored by twenty-two organizations and related to the National Council of Churches of Christ.

Also continued were the placement of United Methodists on NCCC radio programs and in the four-denominational *Protestant Hour.* UMCom co-operated with several denominations in SandCastles for radio programming. For seven years United Methodists were partners with American Lutherans in producing *Scan,* a radio show for young people (and a casualty of the financial cutback of 1982). UMCom promoted placement on radio of another youth-oriented program, *The Place.*

While programming for radio and television, UMCom was also trying to help the viewing/listening public evaluate programs and turn the dial selectively. Notable were the work of the Media Action Research Center (MARC), the program of "Television Awareness Training" and a ground-breaking curriculum, *Growing With Television* (Chapter 14).

A Continuing Question

As ways were found to expand the church's presence in television, staff and commission members were called upon to struggle with questions that had faced TRAFCO from its early days and could never be resolved with a "right" or "wrong" answer. Is the mission of the church in television (and radio) to serve the church by speaking to its own members and winning good will for the church as an institution? Or is it to "be" the church in a public arena, ministering to the public without talking about the church?

The answer always has been "some of each." Spencer and Tower had a vision of the church being in witness to a broad public through the media, and Price, as head of the Public Media Division of UMCom, has continued to press for that view of programming.

In TRAFCO days, programs such as *The Way, Talk Back* and *Breakthru* on television and *Night Call* on radio undertook to help individuals in their own lives with ethical and moral values without talking about the church. More recently the same motive has

114

underlain such programs as *Begin With Goodbye, Learning to Live,* the children's TV spots and *Six American Families.*

On the other hand *Catch the Spirit* has been more direct in presenting the church as a force for good in society and calling attention to United Methodist ministries. It is forthrightly United Methodist and some segments present the church in a way that is sometimes called pre-evangelism.

In a staff memorandum as he left his position in the Public Media Division early in 1990, Price stated the tension between the two approaches against the background of his thirty years with TRAFCO and UMCom. He wrote:

"If we operate in both fields we can make a significant contribution to the life of the church—and the lives of radio and television audiences. If we restrict ourselves simply to 'helping the church tell its story' and not help the church in its mission through the media, we will have failed the church and not risen to our responsibility. . . .

"We simply have to 'be' the church as well as an agency 'of' the church. The issue for me is: are we both servants of the Church and also the Servant Church? Our tradition and our disciplinary authorization call for us to be both."

As the 1990s begin, The United Methodist Church is solidly engaged in television. But, along with the philosophical question, the perennial problem of funding has not gone away. UMCom's television money pays production costs for twenty-six to thirty *Catch the Spirit* programs a year but not for the desired three series of thirteen. A limited amount of money is left for marketing.

Production costs continue to rise. Programs can be given free to cable systems or broadcast stations, but there is little money to purchase time, and every year free television time shrinks.

Problems remain, but the United Methodist who turns on TV can, in fact, see the Cross and Flame there.

·11·

Producer for the Church

*T*hrough the years UMCom continued the TRAFCO role as producer of audiovisuals for the church. The work was done by the Division of Production and Distribution and served local church needs for resources for Christian education, interpretation and general interest programs.

All of the general agencies of The United Methodist Church have made use of UMCom's production services, although they are not required to do so. Agencies are free to do their own production or contract it out; the UMCom staff has had to earn the "business" they receive from United Methodist agencies.

And earn it they have. The studios, editing rooms and sound lab have been kept busy with motion pictures, filmstrips and video—not only for United Methodist clients but on many occasions for other denominations and ecumenical bodies.

During the first quadrennium as UMCom, 1973-76, there were 300 productions for United Methodist general agencies, fourteen annual conferences, a district, a jurisdiction, two church-related colleges and five secondary schools, and the Religious Public Relations Council. The four-year output included twenty-three 16mm color motion pictures, numerous filmstrips, television spot announcements and newsclips, cassette tapes, phonograph records, sound sheets, and 15-frame filmslips.

There was a major film to interpret the World Service Fund.

Produced for the Public Media Division were *Magic Circle*, a three-film package targeted for public schools to train children in conflict management, and *Learning to Live*, an eight-film series to improve interpersonal communication.

Historical films on the occasion of the 1976 two hundredth anniversary of the American Revolution were *Burning Bright*, a historical movie; *The People Called Methodist*, a motion picture celebrating Methodism around the world; and a set of two filmstrips of biographies of United Methodist founders.

Four years later the Division of Production and Distribution reported 350 productions.

Two films for benevolence interpretation were *One in the Lord*, showing a dozen ethnic churches across the country, and *Hope for Life*, filmed under hazardous conditions in Egypt, Lebanon and Israel to show Christianity in the Middle East. For the General Board of Discipleship and General Board of Global Ministries, two films on hunger were produced and for the Committee on Curriculum Resources, multimedia kits on the sacraments of the church. Films on the work of the United Methodist Committee on Relief were shot in Kenya and Thailand.

A Trend Toward Video

As the trend from film to video took hold, UMCom's first major videotape was an award-winning example of video's flexibility. It was *Bookstory*, done for the United Methodist Publishing House with Roger L. Burgess, then a UMPH vice president, as executive producer. UMCom's C. B. Anderson acted a leprechaun-like role to tell the publisher's story. The picture of his antics was shrunk to miniature size and inserted into normal size scenes.

During 1981-84 UMCom initiated two notable learning resources for adults: *A Question of Intimacy*, featuring the well-known Christian writer, Keith Miller, and *The Care and Maintenance of a Good Marriage*, featuring the Rev. O. Dean Martin, pastor and counselor.

The year 1984 brought the bicentennial of American Methodism as dated from the Christmas Conference of 1784. An impressive set of audiovisual resources was produced for a number of church boards, the United Methodist Bicentennial Committee, and the Pan-Methodist Bicentennial Committee—the latter representing several denominations in the Methodist family. Centerpiece was a film/video, *From the Word Go*, with author Alex Haley conducting a tour of ministries addressing the frontiers of 1984. Issued separately as a short film/video was *Clayride*, a segment excerpted from the longer film to take viewers on "a gallop through Methodist history" using "claymation"—animation of clay figures. *From the Word Go* was issued also with English subtitles (for the hearing impaired) and Spanish subtitles. A music video, *A Gift of Song*, featured five choirs from churches in the Methodist heritage.

Also produced in 1984 was *Growing Through Grief*, a six-program video series led by Howard Clinebell, professor of pastoral psychology and counseling at Claremont School of Theology. It was designed to help viewers cope with loss and reach out to others with unhealed grief. Subsequently the video was used, along with a telephone presence of Dr. Clinebell, in teleconferences to train pastors and health care professionals. Peggy J. West considered it "one of the most useful resources we've ever produced."

In 1986 the production facilities were upgraded for the new television show, *Catch the Spirit*. Production staff was enlarged and free-lance technicians employed for the massive assignment of a half-hour weekly show. Portions of the shows were studio shots; some were location shooting by UMCom crews; and others were tapes submitted by field producers at various places.

A major project 1985-88 was a 34-part Bible study series, *Disciple*, produced for the United Methodist Publishing House. There was a six-part series to help parents with nurturing skills, *Parenting: Growing Up Together. In Defense of Creation* was produced to help the church study the bishops' pastoral letter on the nuclear crisis. Also notable was *Questions of Faith*, a six-part video in which prominent thinkers responded to critical issues.

The pace continued. In 1989 a second series of *Questions of Faith* was produced while the first series continued in circulation (and was sold to the U. S. Army for use by chaplains). *Questions of Faith*

118

II featured such diverse Christian thinkers as Bishop Desmond Tutu of South Africa, theologian Rosemary Radford Ruether, and United Methodist Bishop Roy Sano. *Questions of Faith II* proved to be the best selling, most used audiovisual resource UMCom had ever produced. Some annual conferences reported all of their copies of each of the six titles in a set in use at one time.

UMCom teams in 1989 continued to produce the weekly *Catch the Spirit* shows. UMCom joined with Trinity Church, New York, to produce twenty-six *Faces on Faith* programs, made for use on the VISN cable television network and then distributed as an audiovisual resource by EcuFilm. The interviews that were videotaped for *Faces on Faith* received dual use when, with different editing, they became *Questions of Faith II*.

Also produced for showing on VISN was a 50-minute music special with roots in the Black church. For the National Council of Churches UMCom produced *La Lucha*, a television special on the role of the church in Central America, broadcast over ABC-TV.

To do all this, and more, including nine videos to interpret benevolence funds in the new quadrennium, UMCom production crews traveled to China, Brazil, El Salvador, Costa Rica, Guatemala, Malaysia, Indonesia, Jamaica, Puerto Rico, and twenty-three states.

And the first live uplink went from Studio A to a satellite high overhead for national distribution over the Cokesbury Satellite Television Network. It was a one-and-a-half-hour satellite video teleconference for the United Methodist Publishing House's Creative Teaching Series. One hour dealt with creative ways to teach pre-school children in Sunday school, followed by a half-hour of telephone call-ins from viewers.

Distributing the Product

In the early TRAFCO years distribution was not seen as a prime responsibility. Some clients, such as the Board of Missions and the Commission on Promotion and Cultivation, had their own methods of distribution. Others used a film distribution network

119

maintained by the publishing house. The latter was the primary channel for curriculum resources, produced jointly by the house and the Board of Education.

But some of the products were TRAFCO's own, and some clients who had few audiovisuals needed help in distribution. So modestly and gradually TRAFCO got into distribution, and in 1962 a Department of Audiovisual Distribution was set up.

In the early 1970s most film rentals were by the United Methodist Publishing House through regional distribution centers related to its Cokesbury retail network. Cokesbury served churches directly and also was a channel to resource centers developed by annual conferences. But by 1975 the house tired of a responsibility that seemed vaguely related to its task of selling books and other printed resources, and it dropped its film distribution service. United Methodist Communications moved to meet the need by creating a full-service distribution unit: United Methodist Film Service. It was conceived as a single point for information, sales and rental, with titles from several church agencies.

Head of the film service was Wilford V. Bane, a Texan who had come to Nashville to work with audiovisuals for the Board of Education. He moved to TRAFCO to work in education, then was asked to take over distribution. He reached an agreement with a private firm, Mass Media Ministries, that brought success in sales. He continued to direct the work until succeeded by Furman York—formerly of Mass Media Ministries. (While director of AV media production in 1988-90 Bane was loaned by UMCom to head the newly formed VISN television consortium.)

United Methodist Film Service made direct sales and rentals, but was also a wholesaler. It supplied filmstrips and movies, later video cassettes, to a growing network of annual conference resource services—then called film libraries, now media centers.

In 1982, at the suggestion of Dr. Peggy West, Bane made a proposal to other denominations that resulted in EcuFilm. United Methodist Film Service was broadened to provide film and video distribution for Presbyterians, the United Church of Christ, Disciples, and others. Within a year it was averaging 650 rentals a month.

EcuFilm continued to be operated by UMCom, and by 1990 it consolidated video and film resources of the Christian Churches (Disciples of Christ), the Episcopal Church, the Evangelical Lutheran Church in America, the Maryknoll Missioners, the National Council of Churches of Christ in the U.S.A., the Presbyterian Church (U.S.A.), the United Church of Christ, The United Methodist Church, and the World Council of Churches (U.S. Office).

During this time video grew rapidly as the medium of choice for local church use. While the word "film" continued in common speech and in the name EcuFilm, by 1990 video cassettes accounted for a major part of EcuFilm's distribution.

In these ways UMCom could offer to the church an integrated audiovisual service. It could begin with the first concept; move through script, production and manufacturing (one step that has to be contracted out); and then get the finished product into the hands of the user.

·12·

For the Sake of All

All persons are important because they are human beings created by God and loved through and by Jesus Christ. . . . We therefore support social climates in which human communities are maintained and strengthened for the sake of every person."

These words from the United Methodist Social Principles (*The Book of Discipline*, 1988, ¶71) are a guide to the church in all its activities. They are a guide for United Methodist Communications.

UMCom also is governed by policies that apply to all church agencies and institutions: "[to] fulfill their duties and responsibilities in a manner which does not involve segregation or discrimination on the basis of race, color, age, sex, or handicapping condition" (*Discipline*, ¶815).

The communication agency is grateful for this support in the official rule book of the church, but its understanding of the Gospel is such that it would follow these principles even if they were not in *The Book of Discipline*. In fact the forerunners of UMCom were operating "for the sake of every person" long before those words appeared in the *Discipline*.

To serve for the sake of all means to UMCom that its products and services shall be available to all segments of church and society; that its publications, films and other products shall treat all persons with respect and acknowledge their contributions; and that staff and membership on the General Commission on Communication and its committees shall reflect the ethnic diversity of The United Methodist Church.

From the Start

In 1940 membership of the first Commission on Public Information included a Black magazine editor. By 1944 the Rev. Daniel L. Ridout joined the staff part-time as "representative to the Negro press." He distributed news stories of the church to the flourishing Black press and channeled news of the then-segregated Central Jurisdiction into general publications.

Methodist Information developed a network of Black news writers and maintained special services to the Central Jurisdiction until it was integrated with other jurisdictions in 1968. In addition to Black news writers, Methodist Information (and subsequently United Methodist News Service) had Charlotte O'Neal as its New York office manager for twenty-nine years. Agency policy called for full and fair treatment of the news of individuals and churches of all ethnic minorities within the denomination.

TRAFCO practiced racial inclusiveness by monitoring content of its films and by training ethnic minority persons. Internships gave a start in filmmaking to Peter Francis, Charles Washburn, Ruth Villavincencio, Jeff Hirota, Samuel Murillo and others. Often ethnic minority interns were offered staff positions but usually they did not stay long. Such a person with film experience was highly desired in Hollywood or New York and commercial salary offers were far beyond the TRAFCO budget. But TRAFCO and its successor divisions could take credit for giving them a start and that was never forgotten by the trainees.

One of the intern "alumni," Stanley Nelson, later produced an award-winning film on a noted Black businesswoman. Jeff Hirota, who interned at UMCom 1978-79 after study at the film school of New York University, moved into commercial filmmaking as an animator and editor. Later he earned a theology degree and worked in the Interfaith Media Center at Claremont, California. For a time

123

he was partner in a not-for-profit production company and did some free-lance work for UMCom.

TRAFCO in 1970 joined other denominations in producing four one-minute radio spots in Spanish and seven in the Navajo language. The latter were recorded by Navajos at Ganado, Arizona, and dealt with personal struggles such as alcoholism, unemployment and the need for education. They were a test of radio as a medium of communication in an oral culture.

The Wesley film with a Spanish sound track also was released in 1970.

The Chicago labor market provided the Commission on Promotion and Cultivation with employees of many ethnic backgrounds: Black, Hispanic, Korean, Japanese and Chinese. For years Fumiko Matsushita was office administrator and Frederica Westbrooke managed fulfillment services. Thomas Adams and Rita Strong were department directors. The Rev. Warren M. Jenkins of South Carolina worked in business management and field service, later becoming field representative for the Northeastern Jurisdiction. When a committee was established to give oversight to *The Methodist Story*, Bishop M. Lafayette Harris was its first chair.

All three of the predecessor agencies were sensitive to ethnic concerns in their products, services and staffing. All three recruited ethnic minority persons for their governing boards and committees—not as numerous as are found today, but exemplary at the time.

In the Evangelical United Brethren Church the constituency contained few ethnic minority persons, hence their absence from communication staff positions. However, care was taken in publications to cultivate inclusive attitudes and avoid stereotypes.

A UMCom Priority

Since the establishment of United Methodist Communications in 1972, inclusiveness has been a priority. An early act (1974) was to establish an affirmative action program with goals and timelines for employment not only of ethnic minority persons but also for women and persons with handicapping conditions. The program continues and a monitoring committee makes regular affirmative action reports to the general secretary and the commission. By 1988 the UMCom staff was 30 percent ethnic minority persons.

Agency policy today calls for more than ethnic diversity in staff. All audiovisual products and broadcast programs are monitored to assure inclusiveness and avoid stereotypes. Printed materials receive similar scrutiny.

From the start of *Catch the Spirit*, panels were formed to review the previous year's programs for inclusiveness. The 1989 panel found increases in the number of stories about ethnic minority persons, persons of all ages, and those with handicapping conditions. The program is closed captioned for persons with a hearing impairment.

Where language is a factor, as with the Hispanic and Korean communities, printed publications and sometimes film soundtracks are provided. Care is taken to seek ethnic applicants for internships and scholarships, such as the Stoody-West Fellowship. The Perryman Scholarship is explicitly for ethnic minority students.

The Periodical Publications Study of 1975 contained a strong policy statement on meeting the communication needs of ethnic minorities and encouraging self-expression. It declared an obligation for the church to provide communications in languages other than English.

For twelve years the denomination focused on the ethnic minority local church as a "missional priority." For four years, 1977-80, this concern shared the spotlight with two others. From 1981 through 1988 it was the only missional priority. While the entire agency was committed to the priority, the Division of Program and Benevolence Interpretation had major responsibility. P&BI interpreted the priority to church members and promoted financing.

The division, in collaboration with committees that had been set up for the priority, planned national and regional consultations. Training was provided for annual conference leadership in support of the priority. Resources included films, filmstrips and videotapes;

packets, booklets, brochures and posters; news and feature stories; and extensive coverage in *The Interpreter*. There were special sections in *The Interpreter* and tabloid supplements placed in conference papers. A major film, released in 1978, was *One in the Lord*. The Rev. Readus J. Watkins was executive producer, and Edgar A. Gossard producer—a Black and White combination.

Black Staff Members

Black persons, as the most numerous ethnic minority in The United Methodist Church, have been represented in largest numbers in the staff. There have been two Black associate general secretaries: Dr. Watkins for the Division of Program and Benevolence Interpretation, 1977-85, and Newtonia Harris (later Coleman) for administration since 1985. Among others have been the Rev. Hilly Hicks, co-host for *Catch the Spirit*; Laura Okumu, editor of *The Interpreter*; Charles Hightower, John W. Coleman, Jr., and Pamela Watkins Crosby in promotional work; Joseph Whitfield, Stanley Nelson, Peter Francis and Charles Washburn, television, radio and film producers; Paula C. Watson and Roderick Hargo in field service; Louise V. Gray, Garlinda Burton and Denise Hawkins in news service; and Caroline Burns as an administrator. Numerous Black persons have worked as secretaries and in other supporting positions.

Black commission members have made noteworthy contributions to the work of UMCom. Among them have been Harry L. Johnson, who played a major role in planning the Television Presence and Ministry; Newtonia Harris Coleman, who for a brief term was secretary of the commission prior to joining the staff; Lenora C. Stephens, an educator in communications; and the Rev. Cornish Rogers of the faculty of the School of Theology at Claremont.

Special projects with the Black community have been developed in consultation with the caucus, Black Methodists for Church Renewal. For several years editorial assistance was given for *Now*, the newspaper of BMCR. Some UMCom training events have been planned with and for Black participants.

The Hispanic Community

Hispanics, the second largest ethnic group, have special needs because of language. Counsel to UMCom and leadership in communications for Spanish-speaking United Methodist churches has been provided by the Junta Consultiva de Comunicaciones (Consultative Committee on Communications). But Hispanics have been active on the commission and staff as well.

The Rev. Roy D. Barton of Texas served on the original Joint Committee on Communications and chaired its structure committee. He later returned to the commission and was vice-president 1985-88. For a number of years he chaired the junta. Among other Hispanic commission members have been Professor Felix Gutierrez of the University of Southern California; the Rev. Elizabeth Lopez Spence of New Mexico; Carlos Verdecia, one of the editors of the Miami *Herald*; and Mary Silva of the Rio Grande Conference.

Staff persons have included the Rev. Finees Flores, editor of *El Intérprete* 1973-86 and also account executive for promotion of some of the benevolence funds; Edith Delgado LaFontaine of Puerto Rico, his successor as editor; Guillermo Debrot, Bilha Alegria and Magdalena Garcia, editors and translators; and Sam Murillo, who began as an intern in radio and film production, then became producer of the radio show, *Connection*. Others have worked in secretarial and support positions, especially where bilingual skills are required.

The Division of P&BI has long produced promotional resources in Spanish. It began with Human Relations Day, an offering first received in 1973. World Service leaflets in Spanish were added in 1977 and One Great Hour of Sharing materials in 1978. Additional promotional materials in Spanish were issued in later years, including the 1989-92 promotional system, *Come, Share, Rejoice*.

The junta requested and provided personnel for General Conference interpretation, beginning in 1976. The services include a recorded Spanish news summary through InfoServ, audio tape news feeds for radio, and press releases to Spanish-language papers.

A major communication instrument for Hispanic United

Methodists is *El Intérprete*, whose story is told in Chapter 13. It was founded in 1958 as a Spanish edition of *The Interpreter* and has been guided by La Junta Consultiva de Comunicaciones. It fills a role parallel to *The Interpreter*, but most of the content is created originally in Spanish.

The junta began as an editorial committee for the magazine, having its first meeting in Miami in 1958. After formation of UMCom, with its holistic approach to the entire field of communication, the junta in 1975 was restructured to match the concerns of UMCom. Membership was enlarged to assure representation by persons of Mexican, Puerto Rican and Cuban background and to provide geographical representation.

At the request of, and with assistance by, the junta, UMCom produced radio spot announcements in Spanish and reissued filmstrips with Spanish sound tracks. (The radio spots continued a tradition begun in 1970 when TRAFCO joined four other denominations in producing a set of four one-minute spots.) Promotional resources were issued in Spanish. A series of workshops in 1980-81 trained Hispanic persons from each of the five jurisdictions and Puerto Rico in communication skills. It was followed, 1981-85, by a similar series that trained between fifty and seventy-five persons in production for cable television.

A major survey was carried out in 1983 to determine the communication needs of Hispanic churches. Findings were given to the General Commission on Communication and were shared with representatives of all general agencies of the denomination at a three-day meeting in Dallas in January 1984. That gathering spurred new interest on the part of other agencies in producing print and audiovisual resources in Spanish.

The survey revealed minimal communication and public relations activity by Hispanic local churches. To deal with that problem a design team projected a new and larger training program. Funding was provided by the General Council on Ministries from the Missional Priority Fund.

A week-long training session in Nashville, followed by a refresher a year later, prepared six three-person teams (one for each jurisdiction and one for Puerto Rico). Those teams were responsible for conducting at least three workshops in their territory, dispersed so as to be accessible to every Spanish-speaking United Methodist church. In twenty workshops from 1983 to 1985, training was given to 414 persons from 147 churches. The result was not only increased activity in the churches but the continuing influence of the trained communicators.

The junta has proposed a film on the Hispanic United Methodist heritage as a tool for evangelism and educating church members. It is to be made in Spanish with a separate edition with subtitles or sound track in English—the reverse of the usual procedure. Funding has been difficult and the film has been delayed, but the commitment to do it remains.

Among leaders of the junta have been Dr. Barton, LaFontaine, the Rev. Julio Gómez, Leah Gallardo, the Rev. José Borbon, the Rev. Victor Bonilla, Luis Loredo, Alicia Fils-Aime and Carlos Verdecia.

Native Americans

Navajo people in the Southwest received radio messages on moral values in their own language in 1970. TRAFCO was involved in producing these seven one-minute spot announcements through the Fellowship of Navajo Christian Mission, representing five denominations.

In the late 1970s Gene Carter began consulting with a communication committee that had been formed by a United Methodist group called Native American International Caucus (NAIC). The committee was headed by Lee Lonetree Mrotek, a Winnebago from Wisconsin. Assessing needs of Native American United Methodists, the committee concluded that widely scattered members in 158 churches, many of them isolated, needed a newspaper to communicate with one another. Such a paper could also be a voice for Native American concerns in the church at large. A grant from UMCom paid for a pilot issue with Mrotek as editor. It was called *Echo of the Four Winds* and began regular publication in 1981 as a bimonthly tabloid.

The paper met a need, though not without a struggle for acceptance among all of the disparate groups. The Oklahoma Indian Missionary Conference contained half of all United Methodist Native Americans, and it had its own conference paper. *Echo* was readily accepted by the dispersed congregations and gradually won acceptance in Oklahoma as well. It has been a factor, along with the work of the caucus, in building unity within the Native American community and voicing deeply felt concerns.

Mrotek edited the paper, with assistance from the Wisconsin Conference communication staff, until poor health forced her to give it up in 1983. Melba Abrams, wife of a Seneca living in California, succeeded her as editor. As of 1990 assistance in publication is given by the *United Methodist Reporter* in Dallas, and UMCom continues to have a consulting role. Circulation is 3,200.

Because of the heritage of an oral culture, it was determined that the paper should be supplemented by video communication. With NAIC leadership and UMCom staff assistance, a video project was developed. A grant by GCOM of missional priority money enabled the purchase of a video camera, recorder and auxiliary gear for each of the five NAIC regions and training of one person in each region. A week of training was given in October 1984 at Oklahoma City University, and the five video agents began making pictures of church activities that could be shown locally, exchanged with other regions and used in evangelism.

UMCom producers served as consultants in 1984 for a curriculum video, *The Good Mind*. The picture deals in a sensitive way with Native American traditional religion and its relationship to Christianity.

Among leaders in Native American communications, in addition to Mrotek and Mrs. Abrams, have been the Rev. Marvin Abrams, Seneca of California and president of the Native American International Caucus; the Rev. Roy I. Wilson, Cowlitz from Washington state; the Rev. Simeon Cummings and the Rev. Sam Wynn, Lumbees of North Carolina; the Rev. Harry Long, Muskogee Creek of Oklahoma and Arizona; Becky Thompson, Creek of Oklahoma; and Cynthia Abrams, Seneca of California, who has a university degree in journalism.

Native American commission members have been the Rev. Noah Long of Oklahoma, Grace Lowry of South Carolina, Blair A. Gilbert of Pennsylvania, and Russell Coker of Oklahoma. There have been a few Native American interns, and for a time one Native American held a professional editorial position.

Asian Americans

While persons of Asian descent had worked in the staff of UMCom and its predecessors, there was no formal relationship with the church's Asian American community until the late '70s.

The National Federation of Asian American United Methodists undertook its first national convocation to bring together United Methodists whose cultural heritage was from China, Japan, Korea, India, or elsewhere in Asia and the Pacific Islands. Gene Carter of UMCom collaborated with the caucus in planning the convocation, held in San Francisco in December 1978. There was a strong communication component, including press and television coverage of the convocation and workshops to train the Asian American United Methodists to communicate better in their communities.

The Rev. Don E. Collier of the Division of Program and Benevolence Interpretation succeeded Carter as liaison person. In consultation with Korean leadership within the Asian Caucus, the division issued Korean editions of selected promotional resources. World Service leaflets had been the first, in 1977. Other resources in Korean were developed.

The caucus newsletter, *Asian American News*, received assistance from UMCom 1984-88. A Korean program journal, parallel to *The Interpreter* and *El Intérprete*, made its debut early in 1990. The first editor was Jungrea H. Chung. The journal is called *United Methodist Family*.

At the 1980 General Conference, and again in 1984 and 1988, the news room had a Korean desk, providing news and pictures to Korean-language newspapers in the United States.

Four Korean videotapes were produced for UMCom in 1984 by the Interfaith Media Center at Claremont, California, describing

131

The United Methodist Church. A 1989 video, *Welcome Home,* featured the National Federation of Asian American United Methodists and how it offered a "home" to its constituents.

Asian American staff persons have included Dani Aguila, art and design director for a number of years; Fumiko Matsushita, longtime administrative assistant for the P&BI Division and its predecessor agencies; and Zion Huang, assistant director of management information systems. Among those serving as members of the General Commission on Communication have been Stephen Kim, Helen Chang and Sharon Maeda.

The Role of Women

The UMCom story also is a story of increasing participation by women at professional and executive levels.

Apart from the all-male Commission on Public Information in its earliest years, women have always been members of the committees and commissions that have governed the work of communications. Church policy has seen to that. Women have participated actively and given leadership to numerous committees and task forces, but no woman has ever headed the top governing body of UMCom or its predecessors. Barbara Blackstone, a university professor of communication in Pennsylvania, was vice president 1981-84. A number of women have chaired the committees for UMCom's three divisions—in 1990 all three chairs are women.

Maud Turpin (Chapter 2) is a shining example of a woman who was creative, thoroughly professional, and a pioneer in church-related communication at a time when few women enjoyed such a career. But when she retired she was replaced by a man. Mary James Duner briefly headed the Chicago Methodist Information office, and Nadine Callahan (Simpson) wrote news with Arthur West in Chicago. But most of the news writing was done by men until Martha Man came to New York as news writer in 1974. When the next year she was promoted to director of News Service, Frances Smith was added to the New York staff.

By 1990 the professional writers of United Methodist News Service numbered three women and two men.

Sue Couch came early to TRAFCO, working in several areas and making a major contribution as public relations director for TRAFCO and later for UMCom. From 1977 to 1982 the public relations spot was filled by Lyndell D. Smith.

Kay Henderson Cottrell made her mark as a film producer with TRAFCO and later in UMCom. She produced a large number of curriculum resources and made some of the early films lifting up women's concerns in the church. Among those was *Women, Amen*, done in 1974 for the Women's Division of the General Board of Global Ministries. Another woman with extensive film credits is Meredith Underwood.

Women have held the post of managing editor of *The Methodist Story* and *The Interpreter* most of the years since 1964. The line includes Joretta Eppley Purdue (twice), Anna Marie Pritts and Jane Cavey. And in 1988 Okumu became editor. LaFontaine, the editor of *El Intérprete*, has held that post since 1987. Since 1986 primary responsibility for layout design of both magazines has been with Suzanne Sloan, associate art director, later magazine art director.

Barbara Dunlap-Berg joined the promotional materials editorial staff in 1979 and became editorial director in the Division of Program and Benevolence Interpretation in 1981. Assistant editorial director and account executive is Crosby, who joined the staff in 1986. Other women in executive positions in that division and its predecessors have been Cecelia McClure, account executive; Ruth Babcock, art director; Joan F. Babbitt in print production; and Ruth D. Fuller in editorial work. Linda Beher was director of print production and distribution in Evanston for several years, beginning in 1974.

In 1990 the highest ranking women on the staff are the treasurer and two associate general secretaries. The financial officer's post has been held by a woman since 1976 when Anna Conley came, and since 1977 by Peggy W. Welshans. Peggy J. West has headed the Division of Production and Distribution since 1979 and Newtonia Harris Coleman has been associate general secretary for administration since 1985.

Two innovative departments are led by women. Susan Peek has been director of management information systems and its predecessor (data processing). Woodey McEachern has been director of InfoServ since 1980, at which time Anne Gulley became associate director.

Shirley Whipple Struchen, after a career in the Public Media Division, became director of the Office of Conference Services and Communication Education in 1989. The field staff, as expanded at that time, included two women: Deanna K. Armstrong joined Paula C. Watson who had been a field staff consultant since 1977.

As of the 1989 affirmative action report, women outnumbered men on the staff by eighty-seven to fifty. At executive levels men outnumbered women, but 48 percent were female, slightly exceeding the goal. Sixty percent of professional positions were held by women, well above the half-and-half goal.

An Unfinished Story

Affirmative action includes persons with handicapping conditions. Through the years UMCom and its predecessors have been sensitive to employment of persons with physical handicaps. As they have contributed to the tasks and the development of UMCom, several of the staff have served as role models for others in overcoming obstacles.

A sheltered workshop for adults with mental handicaps has done contract work for UMCom, giving employment in tasks such as assembling packets.

In the monitoring of all products—film, video and print—producers and editors are careful to avoid stereotypes and to present all persons in terms of their intrinsic worth, not physical limitations. Films, articles and TV program segments have dealt with issues around the treatment of persons with handicapping conditions.

The history of United Methodist Communications' relationships with ethnic minorities, women and persons with handicapping conditions is not a perfect story. There has been frustration that affirmative action goals could not always be met. Persons with professional level communication skills are not easily found in all desired groups. Despite training sessions to sensitize staff against racism and sexism, relationships have sometimes fallen short of the ideal. Projects that have been planned by UMCom staff and the consultative bodies have not always been funded or staffed as fully as desired.

Yet in spite of occasional shortfalls, the will is there. United Methodist Communications has set its goals to live out in the world of the media the Gospel principle that all persons are important and that the work of UMCom should be "for the sake of every person."

·13·

Publishing the Good News

The Apostle Paul wrote. Matthew, Mark, Luke and John were writers. The early Christians wrote, copied manuscripts, and circulated them by the technology of the day.

Biblical scholar Edgar J. Goodspeed notes that early Christians "sought not only by deed and word, but by all the most advanced techniques of publication to carry the gospel, in its fullness and without reserve, to all mankind."

The activity may have slowed at times, but it never stopped. Advances in technology—from Gutenberg to the latest computer-controlled, high-speed, color offset press—have been used by Christians. Publishing activities by United Methodist Communications are a part of that line.

Print has been a mainstay of the work of UMCom and its predecessor bodies. This is true despite the explosive increase of television, radio and computer-based communication. The printed word has its own place as a message that can be distributed conveniently, can be picked up at a time of the reader's choice, and can be stored, copied and passed along. The printed word has permanence.

And just as the new media reinforced the printed message, so print supports the message in the electronic media. Each has its function, and they must be used together in a holistic approach to the communication task.

136

This chapter tells how UMCom has used magazines, newsletters, books, and occasional ventures into educational curriculum. The full story of print would include more: pamphlets, posters, leader's guides—even printing on shirts and balloons.

The Program Journals

The first program journal in what is now The United Methodist Church was *Spotlight*, started by the Evangelical United Brethren in 1955. The first issue, July-August, announced its purpose "to promote the total program of Christian education and evangelism."

At the outset, *Spotlight* was sponsored by EUB Men, the Board of Christian Education and the Board of Evangelism. It was edited by staff of the sponsoring agencies. It replaced three publications and was sent free to pastors and conference leaders in the three fields. Usual issues were twenty-four pages and the content was program ideas and resources for education, evangelism and men's work.

In 1963 *Spotlight* came under sponsorship of a new co-ordinating agency known as the Program Council. Frequency was switched to quarterly, pages were added, and content broadened to concerns of all program agencies. Editorial tasks continued to be shared. The guiding hand was that of the Rev. Paul V. Church, general secretary of the Council of Administration and originator of the concept of the Program Council within the Council of Administration.

The last issue of *Spotlight* was for April-June 1968, just before it was combined with *The Methodist Story*.

On the Methodist side *The Methodist Story* began in March 1957. It had been authorized by the 1956 General Conference in response to demand for consolidation of program/promotional magazines published by various boards of the church. The new program journal was successor to five of them (Chapter 6).

Responsibility was assigned to the Commission on Promotion and Cultivation and the Rev. E. Harold Mohn was publisher. The first editorial staff consisted of Edwin H. Maynard, editor; Darrell R. Shamblin, managing editor; and James L. Riedy, production manager. Business manager was the Rev. Howard Greenwalt.

Maynard continued as editor until 1967, when he became editorial director. Shamblin became editor, a post he held for *The Methodist Story* and *The Interpreter* for twenty-one years. In 1988 he became associate publisher. Other staff of *The Methodist Story* were Joretta Eppley Purdue and Anna Marie Pritts as managing editors and Edward J. Mikula as art director. At various times the Rev. Warren M. Jenkins and the Rev. Arthur V. Long were business managers. General secretaries in turn were publishers: the Rev. Elliott L. Fisher and Dr. Greenwalt.

The Methodist Story was published eleven times a year at the start, and each issue had thirty-two or more pages. It contained information from all program agencies of the denomination. Each agency was asked to appoint a staff person to an Editorial Council.

The very first issues contained, along with articles, two departments that have continued without interruption, still appearing in *The Interpreter* in 1990. They are "Just Out," brief announcements of new program resources, and "It Worked for Us," in which readers write about successful activities in their churches. The latter won an award from the Associated Church Press (ACP) in 1986.

The Methodist Story from the outset perforated every page to encourage readers to tear out pages and pass them along. Perforation was continued more than twenty-five years. Three-hole punching for storage in a ring binder was begun with Volume 1, Number 1, and continues in *The Interpreter*.

A sound sheet, a light-weight phonograph record bound into the December issue of 1965 in support of TRAFCO's *Man With the Mike* radio show was a first in religious publishing. Sound sheets were repeated several times in later issues.

The Interpreter

Leading up to the union of 1968, staff of *The Methodist Story* met with Dr. Church and others who worked on *Spotlight*. They planned what they proudly announced as the first merged publication for the new church. It appeared at the Uniting Conference in Dallas as *Methodist Story-Spotlight*. In January 1969 it became *The Interpreter*. *The Interpreter* continued the purpose of both its predecessors. The staff was the old *Methodist Story* staff, relocated in Dayton where the united church's Program Council was housed. In that year the Rev. Ralph E. Baker came from conference public relations work in California to be managing editor. He held the post for eight years, then became an associate editor.

Content and appearance of *The Interpreter* were much like the old *Methodist Story*, and the merged publication followed the Methodist pattern of sending it without charge to all pastors and a specified number of local church officials, a mailing list of 340,000. Representatives from the program agencies were continued, eventually being called Editorial Advisory Group.

For a number of years the advisory group met in local churches in various locations to enable dialog with persons who were using the magazine. The meetings yielded such helpful reminders as the case of the Oklahoma layman whose wife put the magazine on his bedside stand—so the editors had to hold his attention as he drifted off to dreams.

Studies of readership were contracted regularly, usually on a four-year cycle. Readability of articles was tested within the staff. There were periodic changes to freshen appearance and keep up with fashions in design. A 1986 redesign won an award from the Associated Church Press. The latest and most striking change in appearance was the addition of four-color printing in every issue beginning in November-December 1988.

With the demise of *United Methodists Today* in 1975, the United Methodist Publishing House offered to edit, print and place in *The Interpreter* a 16-page supplement, "News and Comment." The arrangement terminated after the 1976 General Conference, but UMCom decided to continue the feature and F. Paige Carlin was brought from the publishing house as its editor.

But throughout its history the magazine's main content, as a program journal, has been articles relating to the work of the local church. These articles and columns helpful to persons holding specific church offices were supplied by program boards.

Very useful to churches has been the Program Planning Number, issued annually during most of the magazine's history. The one for 1976, prepared jointly with the General Council on Ministries, was reprinted as a book and used for years as a planning guide. It was issued also in Spanish. Another annual tradition is an issue that features the entire benevolence program of the church.

In 1983 the number of issues per year was reduced from ten to eight. Circulation leveled off at around 300,000.

Staff in later years have included Leonard M. Perryman (Chapter 14) and the Rev. Harold H. Hazenfield as associate editors, Baker variously as managing editor and associate editor, Jane Cavey and Purdue (a second time) as managing editors, and Paul Behrens, William Patterson (contract) and Dani Aguila as art directors. For many years Agnes May Morrison managed editorial production.

Laura Okumu, a graduate of Duquesne and the University of California at Los Angeles, joined the staff in 1983 as an editorial assistant and later was promoted to associate editor, devoting part of her time to promotional assignments. Before coming to *The Interpreter* she had worked with the League of Red Cross Societies in Geneva and had been senior editor for Eastern Africa Publications in Tanzania, editor for Khartoum University Press in Sudan, and on the editorial staff of *East Africa Journal* in Kenya.

In 1988 when Shamblin was promoted into publishing, she became editor. Succeeding publishers were the Rev. Readus J. Watkins, Roger L. Burgess and the Rev. Donald E. Collier.

In Other Languages

The Spanish-language program journal, *El Intérprete*, dates from 1958, when Maynard was sent to Cuba to cover an evangelistic campaign. There he met Miguel Soto, editor of *El Evangelista Cubano*, and they devised a plan for the staff of *The Methodist Story* to send information from its columns to Havana, where Soto selected and translated. Under the Spanish title, "La Historia Metodista," it appeared as a column in *El Evangelista Cubano*, and Soto supplied reprints for stateside Hispanic churches.

Before long the title, awkward in Spanish, was changed to "Acción Metodista." An advisory group of representative Hispanic Methodists was formed (Chapter 12). The reprint version shipped from Cuba to the States was a paper of four or eight magazine-size pages. Soon Castro's revolution led to paper shortages and difficult communications. After a time the papers for mainland distribution stopped coming.

Arrangements were made with a new editor. He was the Rev. Jorge N. Cintrón, in 1964 just completing graduate study in journalism at Syracuse University as a Crusade Scholar. Dr. Cintrón edited part time while a university and seminary professor in Puerto Rico.

Under his editorship *Acción Metodista* was an eight-page paper, magazine size and printed in two colors. Content quickly moved beyond translations from *The Methodist Story*, although program ideas and helps still were selected and translated. Cintrón solicited writers from Hispanic churches in Puerto Rico, New York, Florida, Texas and California.

When the English-language program journal took a new name after church union, the Spanish edition became *El Intérprete*. Cintrón continued as editor for a time, then asked to be relieved.

After a year's hiatus, in 1972 a new advisory committee met in Dallas with representatives from Puerto Rico, New York, Florida, Chicago, California and Texas. The group made plans for renewed publication and advised as to content. They recommended the Rev. Finees Flores as part-time editor.

Dr. Flores, a Texan of Mexican descent, was pastor of Christian Fellowship Church in Chicago. He agreed to edit the magazine, with the Rev. Guillermo Debrot, another Chicago pastor, as managing editor and literary advisor. In 1976 Flores joined the staff full time, taking on duties in promotion.

The original distribution plan for the Spanish magazine was to send bundles to each Spanish-speaking church. Later a subscription list was developed, each church being entitled to a number of free subscriptions according to its membership. By 1980 the circulation was 4,000, rising to 5,500 by 1988.

When offices of the Division of Program and Benevolence

Interpretation were consolidated in Nashville in 1986, Flores opted not to make the move, returning to a pastorate. The new editor was Edith LaFontaine, a Puerto Rican who had served on La Junta Consultiva de Comunicaciones and who had writing and editorial experience in San Juan and New York.

El Intérprete in 1990 was being published six times a year, normally twenty-four pages, in two colors. Writers were drawn from all parts of the Hispanic United Methodist community. The magazine is unique among mainline Protestant denominations.

One more program journal joined the ranks in 1990. It is in the Korean language and is called *United Methodist Family* (Chapter 12). The Rev. Jungrea Chung was chosen as the first editor, working part time while associate pastor of a church in New Jersey.

Newsletters

Newsletters have been viewed with suspicion by church bureaucrats, often obsessed with co-ordination. They decry the "proliferation" of newsletters. But communicators praise the newsletter because it can be tailored to a narrowly defined audience and produced in small quantities at modest cost.

UMCom has taken its own advice. It publishes newsletters.

The earliest was put out by Methodist Information, appearing under various names from 1954 to 1972. First it was *Mine*, then *Share*, and finally *Sharing*. During most of its life it was edited by Arthur West. It was directed primarily to commission members, staff and persons doing conference public relations. It was mimeographed on letter-size paper and continued until United Methodist Information was merged into UMCom.

Continuity was published by TRAFCO, beginning in 1955. It was aimed at commission members, staff and persons doing television, radio and film work in the conferences. During most of its life it was edited by Sue Couch. It reported on new developments in technology, training opportunities, and TRAFCO productions.

Under UMCom the two newsletters were combined and published as *Sharing/Continuity* from 1973 to 1976. Editorial chores were shared by Couch and Thomas S. (Tom) McAnally. Targeted to the audience of its predecessors, *Sharing/Continuity* contained ideas, helps for people working in the conferences, and news about the formation and development of the new communication agency.

Couch for a time was director of public relations for UMCom, working from her old Nashville base. In 1977 it was determined that the PR director should be located in Dayton with the general secretary, and Couch chose to stay in Nashville. At that time Lyndell D. Smith became director of public relations, and she took over as editor of what then was called *UMCommunicator*.

The number of pages and scope of its content were increased. *UMCommunicator* served a growing constituency of professional and volunteer church communicators, educators, and communication professionals in secular fields. For eight years the November issue doubled as the agency's annual report.

After the financial cutback of 1982, *UMCommunicator* was moved to Nashville, along with other public relations functions. In 1983 a new assistant in that department, Brenda Blanton Lane, became editor. After a year and a half her plans were cut short by her tragic death. The newsletter lapsed.

In 1989 a successor to *Communicator* appeared. It is *Network*, edited by Shirley Whipple Struchen and seeking to build networks of communication persons—in UMCom, in the annual conferences, and among interested persons wherever found.

In addition to these agency-wide newsletters, there have been others published by departments for their constituencies. Among them have been *Intercom*, *FYI*, *15 Minutes at UMCom* and *UMCommunity* at various times for UMCom staff; *Resource Rap* about audiovisual resources; *The Link* for Television Presence and Ministry; and *Pep Talk* for radio and television producers.

Book Publishing

A significant book in the communication field was published not by UMCom but by Abingdon Press. Its author was the agency's first staff person, the Rev. Ralph W. Stoody. The book was *A Handbook of Church Public Relations,* published in 1959. For years it was considered the standard work in its field.

The Commission on Promotion and Cultivation published a number of books related to its various assignments during its years as an independent commission.

By far the most successful was *Endless Line of Splendor,* first published in 1950 by the Advance Committee. It was written by Halford E. Luccock, a fabled raconteur, and told Methodist history through anecdotes. It was illustrated by an equally famous artist, Lynd Ward. Because it continued the work of the Advance, the commission held rights to the book and reissued it with slight revisions in 1964. In 1975, after Dr. Luccock's death, some dated material was removed, and the Rev. Webb Garrison wrote twenty-two additional vignettes to bring the record up to date. The aging Ward made ten new drawings. In its three editions the book went through multiple printings and for years was a popular source book of church history.

Two paperback books were authored by staff persons. Greenwalt wrote *Ideas and Helps for the District Superintendent,* 1957, and Maynard wrote *Mission by Choice* for the Advance, 1969.

Christian Strategy for a Struggling World, a symposium for stewardship cultivation, was published in 1959. *One Witness in One World* was written in 1964 by Bishop Roy H. Short for a quadrennial program. It was published also in Spanish.

In 1968, following the tradition of *Endless Line of Splendor,* the commission asked Webb Garrison to write an anecdotal account of work accomplished by Methodist Church benevolence giving. It was titled *Giving Wings to a Warm Heart.* Appendices documented financial contributions for benevolences and their promotion from the union of 1939 to the union of 1968.

Not a book in the same sense as the others, but a major publishing enterprise was *Come, Share, Rejoice,* created by the Division of Program and Benevolence Interpretation under Collier's direction in 1988. It provides in a ring binder indexed information about fourteen benevolence funds and resources to tell their stories. It was sent by P&BI to every pastor, with supplemental pages to be mailed from time to time. It is supported by videotapes with stories relating to the funds.

TRAFCO and the Division of Public Media have published books related to films or TV programs. Notable among those were *Six American Families*, by Paul Wilkes, 1977, and *Begin with Goodbye*, 1980. Each told, in book form, the stories portrayed in its TV series.

Other Uses of Print

In support of its interest in educating church members and the public about use of television, the Division of Public Media was a major partner in founding the Media Action Research Center (MARC). Through MARC the division was a major sponsor of the program of Television Awareness Training (Chapter 14) and the *TAT Manual*. The 300-page manual was edited by Ben Logan. Editions of 1977 and 1979 were used in hundreds of training sessions all over the country.

The division has been involved in other training enterprises that paired films for television and classroom with supporting books. One of those was *Learning to Live*, 1974, based on the "transactional analysis" concept. *The Magic Circle Conflict Curriculum* consisted of a 130-page book and three 12-minute films to help children deal positively with everyday conflicts.

All of the divisions and their predecessor agencies have published numerous training manuals and resources, beginning with Holt McPherson's *Churchmen, Let's Go to Press* in 1950. While the Rev. Thomas H. Nankervis was working in communication education he put out a series of training pamphlets under the whimsical title of *Shoddy Pads*. They covered such topics as clown ministry, outdoor bulletin boards, and audio cassettes.

Since the position of local church co-ordinator of communications was created in 1976, the UMCom staff has been responsible with the start of each quadrennium to write a new "guidelines" book, published as part of a set for all local church officers.

A quarterly journal majoring in critiques of the public media came under partial sponsorship of UMCom. It is *Media & Values*, originated in California by Elizabeth Thoman and described as "a resource for media awareness." The Media Action Research Center (Chapter 14) became publisher and UMCom joined twelve other religious groups on the journal's board of directors.

While UMCom issues publications in many formats, the widest circulation of all undoubtedly is use by newspapers and magazines of releases from United Methodist News Service (UMNS).

The professional news staff in 1990 is made up of Thomas S. McAnally, director since 1983, Robert Lear, M. Garlinda Burton, Linda Bloom and B. Denise Hawkins. These five writers at Nashville, New York and Washington generate more than 500 news stories a year. Computer-controlled mailing lists direct the releases to nearly fifty discrete categories of editors and broadcast news directors according to location and subjects of interest. UMNS operates newsrooms at major church meetings to help media writers do their own stories. The news service also recommends spokespersons for newspaper or magazine interviews and as guests for radio/television talk shows.

The news releases cover activities of the bishops and other leaders of the church as well as the general boards, councils and committees, including some 150 meetings a year. UMNS also reports on activities of annual conferences, local churches and individual Christians where the news is of general interest. Some stories analyze current issues. The number of news reports sent out is not the whole story, according to McAnally. "If our work is to be evaluated by the number of releases," he says, "we could easily double it. Our job is to judge carefully what is news and to send out only what we honestly believe editors will use." That policy has built credibility.

While news releases are distributed by mail, they are accessible to a wide audience by computer through CircuitWriter Network on the NewsNet data base (Chapter 8). Now a weekly summary, "News in Brief," is being placed on the network for editors of local church newsletters.

Somewhere between news releases and newsletters are *Methodists Make News*, sent weekly to 550 U.S. subscribers, and *Highlights* for 300 Methodist editors in other countries. Both serve United

Methodists and other denominations in the Methodist family of churches. A monthly Spanish edition of *Methodists Make News* is to begin in 1990, edited by Julio Gómez.

It is reputed that Martin Luther once hurled his ink pot at the Devil. UMCom may not have been aiming exactly at the Devil, but it has used a vast amount of printer's ink in the process of helping the church do its work and tell its story.

·14·

How to Do It

UMCom is committed to education.

Training persons for the church's work of communication is a job that never is finished. It has been going on since the earliest days of the organization and will continue into the future.

The Book of Discipline directs UMCom to do training, but that is not the reason UMCom does it. A credible job of communication for the church would be impossible without training.

The *Discipline* instruction reads: "It shall provide resources, counsel and staff training for area, conference, and district communication programs and develop guidelines in consultation with persons working in areas, conferences, and districts." (1988, ¶1906.20)

The job actually is bigger than training for work at the conference and district levels. Staff of UMCom itself, while already professionals, need continuing education to keep up with that old revolution. Internships and scholarships are part of the picture. Frequent programs educate the public on media use.

Commitment to Training

It started early. Within a few years of the start of Methodist Information, Ralph Stoody and his staff were creating resources to help congregations with their in-church communication, press releases and public relations. By the late '40s Methodist Information was sending its staff and volunteers into episcopal areas to conduct workshops. Then in 1953 came the first "national staff" gathering, which brought together persons holding PR jobs for conferences or areas (Chapter 4).

Early on TRAFCO also began training programs. One was to sharpen the skills of church persons working in radio and television. In the years 1960-63 some 1,500 persons received training in production, placement and utilization. Large numbers were trained for television shows that involved local panels. For *Talk Back* (1958-60) 7,500 persons were trained and 600 for *Breakthru* (1962).

With growing use of audiovisuals in churches, TRAFCO looked for ways to help make that use as effective as possible. As they came on staff, Sam Barefield and Wil Bane worked on this question. They developed AV utilization seminars, held at widely distributed locations. As time went by the agenda broadened and these became jurisdictional seminars, not just on audiovisuals, but on communication as a whole.

There were occasional national gatherings, such as the 1964 meeting in New York on the communication revolution (Chapter 9). There were three-week summer courses in communication at theological seminaries.

TRAFCO pioneered internships. From its early days TRAFCO saw in-service training as a means to help women and ethnic minority persons gain access to communication jobs. A few of the interns became staff for TRAFCO, but for most it became an entry into the profession.

Training in the Commission on Promotion and Cultivation centered on promotional techniques. The field staff was constantly working with annual conference leaders to help them do better promotion and interpretation. Sometimes their efforts extended to districts and local churches in programs such as Operation Understanding. This program brought a large team, mostly staff of denominational agencies, to speak in every church of a district about the good accomplished with money given for the benevolence funds.

At the national level the commission trained district superintendents and other conference leaders through quadrennial convocations. Sometimes there were also "Mid-Quadrennium Promotional Conferences."

Once the Evangelical United Brethren Church had established its Communication Council, training was identified as a major need. Where conferences expressed interest, workshops were offered with national staff leadership.

Organized to Do the Job

To all of this history, United Methodist Communications was heir. When structure was being devised in 1973, education was given high status in the Division of Research, Education and Liaison (REAL). No matter that the division lacked funding and was abandoned. The commitment was continued in an Office of Communication Education and Field Service that functioned for a time. It was resurrected in 1988 as Office of Conference Services and Communication Education.

During the brief life of REAL and in the office that succeeded it, the Rev. Gene W. Carter was the key person for communication education. While field staff concentrated on training for promotion, Dr. Carter developed a panel of persons with professional skills all over the country and recommended them to conferences for their training needs. Carter led workshops himself.

When the Rev. Thomas H. Nankervis joined the staff he specialized in conducting workshops at varied locations around the country, most of them labeled "national" and centering on particular skills. They covered such topics as newsletters, cartooning, clown-mime-puppet ministries and printed communications. Nankervis coined the name "Bushel Basket Workshops," derived from Jesus' parable about not hiding your light "under a bushel." A 1980 workshop on clown, mime, puppetry and dance in New Orleans was covered in two full pages with color photos by *Time* magazine. The New Orleans workshop and a companion in Ithaca, New York, totaled 750 participants.

To reinforce use of audiovisuals in local churches, encouragement was given to the distribution centers in conferences. The Office of Communication Education and United Methodist Film Service began consultations for directors of Annual Conference Resource Centers. The third, in 1977, was attended by directors from some forty conferences. The agenda had to do with obtaining, storing and distributing films, but more important was the role of the resource center director as counselor of local churches on selection of AV resources and wise use of them—especially in the churches' educational programs. Plans were made for five jurisdictional workshops for center directors.

The calendar for TRAFCO workshops of all kinds for 1977-78 listed more than a dozen scattered from Oregon to Georgia.

Dianne Bowden was added to this staff, specializing in workshops for the editors of church newsletters. Her work was part of the newsletter emphasis in the Comprehensive Communication System growing out of the periodicals study of 1975 and supported by the MasCom Fund. Her program included training leaders to conduct workshops in their areas. Persons accredited at a 1977 training event proceeded to conduct more than fifty district, conference or area workshops on newsletters.

Activities of the '80s

The education program ventured into new electronic media in 1982 with plans for sessions on telecommunications and computers and a "dial-in workshop." But the financial crunch of 1982 terminated the work. It also forced re-evaluation. The outcome was that UMCom no longer conducted many workshops. Instead, it encouraged annual conferences to accept that responsibility, with UMCom providing advice, resources, and sometimes instructors.

Thus, when the Television/Telecommunication Fund in 1985 permitted adding staff for telecommunications, the Rev. Keith A. Muhleman was given conference relationships as a responsibility. That emphasis was continued and strengthened in the assignments given to Shirley Whipple Struchen in 1988.

In 1990 the UMCom field staff, one in each jurisdiction, is expected to help conferences in all aspects of communication, not merely promotion. The Office of Conference Services and Communication Education co-operates with the United Methodist Association of Communicators and jurisdictional fellowships of communicators in their annual sessions that offer continuing education for conference professional communication staff and committee leadership. When requested, staff assists conferences in developing workshops and other training events.

With reorganization and enlargement of the field staff in 1989, the team working under Struchen's direction consisted of Paula C. Watson, the Rev. W. Cannon Kinnard, the Rev. M. Ervin Dailey, Roderick L. Hargo and Deanna K. Armstrong. Each was assigned to one of the church's five jurisdictions.

The gatherings of communication staff from annual conferences, begun by Methodist Information in the '50s, have continued through the years with modifications. After a lapse of some years, in 1978 a National News Consultation was held in Memphis, Tennessee. It was planned by representatives of United Methodist News Service and conference communication staffs.

In recent times it has been the custom to hold a briefing on General Conference issues a year prior to each quadrennial conference. In other years, UMCom helps with continuing education features of the annual meetings of the United Methodist Association of Communicators.

Help for Television Viewers

The role of television as a shaper of values in modern society cries out for responsible use of TV. UMCom has had a continuing interest in national policy and regulation of the industry, frequently adopting position statements and sometimes seeking to influence Congress or regulatory bodies. But the major thrust has been to help individuals and families become more responsible in their own viewing.

152

The instrument has been Television Awareness Training, a program of the Media Action Research Center (MARC).

Nelson Price, as head of the Public Media Division, was one of the founders of MARC and its president. UMCom contributes to MARC's ongoing program and to specific projects.

As an outgrowth of its research into the effects of TV on viewers, MARC created an educational program, Television Awareness Training (TAT). It began in 1977 and continued more than a decade. It was used all across the United States and Canada and, with modifications, was used in other countries. Sponsors were UMCom and units of the Church of the Brethren and American Lutheran Church.

At the inception of TAT, Dr. Price promised: "TAT will provide new information, new experiences of TV viewing, assessment tools for the ways in which persons use television, and alternative actions. It will help turn some negative TV experiences into positive, creative growth experiences."

In the introduction to the TAT *Viewer's Guide*, Ben Logan wrote: "I don't think TV is a monster. . . . But I think if I join the screen carelessly, non-selectively, blindly, then a monster is being created. That relationship between an unthinking screen and a mindless me is monster enough." He then offered the reader clues, starting points and insights for selective, responsible viewing of television.

The TAT program began in January 1977 in Atlanta with three days of training for forty would-be instructors who paid $138 each. For another $750 they received films and texts valued at $1,500, which they might hope to recover by collecting a fee of $20 from each registrant at workshops they conducted. Persons certified as trainers were prepared to conduct local TAT workshops in eight units, which might be stretched out over eight weeks or concentrated into a weekend. Among the units were television violence, television and children, TV advertising, and the values communicated by TV news.

In its first year sixteen leadership training events were attended by 334 persons, of whom 165 were licensed to conduct TAT workshops. Of those, sixty-five were United Methodists. During its first five years TAT certified 511 trainers in forty-four states, and the total later reached 529. Persons who attended their workshops numbered in the thousands, and they purchased 32,000 copies of two editions of the guidebook.

A global impact came from translating the resources into other languages and training leaders in many countries. Printed materials were adapted and translated in whole or in part into Spanish, Portuguese, Italian, German, Japanese and other languages. Logan alone held training sessions in Canada, Barbados, Italy and Brazil. Others led sessions in Japan, Korea and elsewhere. TAT spread further through work of persons who came to America for training, then returned to adapt the program to their homeland. "Learn and then go teach" was the watchword.

Another approach to helping people be responsible television viewers was a five-level curriculum, *Growing With Television*. It was proposed and developed by Peggy West, who wrote the adult level. Price and Logan, working through MARC, got funding from Trinity Parish, New York. The curriculum was designed for use in churches and was approved by the United Methodist Curriculum Committee. It was published by Graded Press and continued in use for years.

Theological Studies

The theological understandings that guide the work of communication have been approached in many ways. TRAFCO sponsored some early conversations on the subject. A paper, "The Gospel to the Multitudes" was written by the Rev. Harry C. Spencer, Bishop Donald H. Tippett, and the Rev. Robert E. Goodrich of Dallas (star of *The Pastor* and later bishop). It was presented to the Council of Bishops in December 1953 as a theological base for TRAFCO's work.

Theological discussion continued in TRAFCO staff meetings, commission sessions and occasional staff papers. William F. Fore in his dissertation traces an evolution from a "pipeline" theory of communication to a view of the media as a place where the church encounters culture and reacts with it. He attributes radical changes in programming in the '60s to the changed theological understandings.

After UMCom was formed, a theologian, the Rev. J. Robert Nelson, was asked to address a 1974 meeting of the Joint Committee on Communications. Dr. Nelson, then dean of Boston University School of Theology, told the committee that "the task of communication is an inherent part of the faith . . . [and] essentially missionary in nature."

UMCom named a task force to develop a theological statement that was adopted in 1975 and influenced the 1976 *Discipline*. The statement saw communication as an essential part of Christian commitment and stressed dialog—both speaking and listening. It has remained in effect, with occasional revision.

The 1987 version, shared with the 1988 General Conference, began with God's communication through creation and incarnation and declared that faithfulness to the communicating God requires Christians to be faithful communicators of God's story. The 1990 version, like its predecessors, calls for proclamation of the Gospel message by use of "the many means of communication that God has made available to us." It lays the responsibility on all Christians. (The complete text appears as Appendix G.)

In 1983, as part of the process leading to the Television/Telecommunication proposal for the 1984 General Conference, there was a Conference on Christianity in Ancient and Modern Media. It was sponsored by UMCom and United Theological Seminary in Dayton. Planning was led by Curtis Chambers, Dean Newell J. Wert and Professor Thomas E. Boomershine. A major resource person was Walter J. Ong, noted Jesuit scholar of theology and communication. Participants were teachers in United Methodist theological seminaries, UMCom staff and commission members, communicators in annual conferences, and representatives of the TV industry. It was hoped to begin formation of a network of persons interested in theology and communications.

The next year a second convocation, involving some of the same persons, was held at the School of Theology at Claremont (California). Planning was led by Peggy West for UMCom and

Professor Steve F. Jackson for the seminary. One of the leaders was Professor John Cobb, a noted proponent of "process theology."

The theological seminaries, as training grounds for clergy, have always been seen as key spots for education in communication. The predecessor agencies and UMCom itself have sent staff to consult with seminary faculty and to teach or recommend guest lecturers.

Interest in theological guidance for the work of communication continues. The hoped-for network has yet to develop.

An endowment was provided at Garrett (now Garrett-Evangelical) Theological Seminary in honor of Dr. Spencer, a Garrett alumnus, upon his 1973 retirement. Initial gifts of more than $13,000 established the fund, whose purpose was to finance lectureships and other programs in communication at the seminary, to provide graduate fellowships, or to finance research.

By June, 1989, the Harry C. Spencer Communication Education Fund at the seminary amounted to more than $75,000. A major use of proceeds from the endowment has been to train faculty and students for use of media in courses and to purchase film and video equipment for classroom use. In 1989-90 the fund financed research by Jeffrey Mahan on the electronic media and the theological curriculum. The Rev. Neal F. Fisher, seminary president, indicated that Dr. Mahan was to lead in developing further use of electronic media in the seminary's own communication, in training pastors to use media, and in the classroom. Work financed by the Spencer Fund was to go alongside program production in a television studio provided to the seminary by a cable TV company.

Continuing Education

For the staff of UMCom there have been occasional seminars or training sessions. These events have helped staff members in such areas as writing, design, and new developments in technology. Another prominent and continuing feature has been seminars, required for all staff to attend, on racism and sexism.

Many staff persons have been sent (at UMCom expense) for

specific training to meet their job needs. Policy for many years has provided tuition help for staff persons who enroll in evening classes at nearby universities. Study leaves of up to four months are offered to professional staff at five-year intervals. Some who have taken advantage of this policy have written useful papers, such as a survey of church public relations offices by Winston H. Taylor. Dr. Chambers used his 1979 leave to study a wide variety of television ministries in the United States and Europe. His paper was part of the background for the Television Presence and Ministry.

Responding to a proposal from the United Methodist Association of Communicators (UMAC), UMCom agreed to be a partner in a program to certify qualified persons in Christian communication. Certification is needed by a candidate for the diaconal ministry in communication. It proved to be of interest to many others as a professional endorsement.

Standards were developed by a joint committee and approved by both sponsoring bodies. The first person certified, in 1980, was J. Fred Rowles of the UMCom staff. The program continues, under supervision of a committee of three persons from each sponsor. As of 1990, sixty-four persons had been certified (Appendix E). Certification is for four years, subject to renewal upon meeting requirements for continuing education.

Aid for Students

Internships have been offered in the agency for many years. Among the forebears, TRAFCO made largest use of interns. This program helped to launch communication careers for a number of ethnic minority persons. The Commission on Promotion and Cultivation used interns occasionally for editorial work on its magazine.

Since the three agencies became UMCom, internships have been policy for the entire agency. Scarce funding and departmental work loads had limited the number of internships, but they received new emphasis during 1985-88. In those four years there were fourteen interns and 70 percent were ethnic minorities or women. Some internships are related to college programs.

157

The best known aid to education for communication has been the Stoody-West Fellowship (Appendix D). This is an award for graduate-level study in some area of communication, honoring two staff pioneers: Ralph W. Stoody and Arthur West.

The fellowship was established in 1964 as the Stoody Fellowship on the occasion of Dr. Stoody's retirement (Chapter 4). The first award was for $1,000 for a year's study. After his 1975 retirement Dr. Arthur West was honored by an award for news writing, first given in 1977. After three awards the writing prize was dropped and in 1981 the fellowship became "Stoody-West." (One factor in the change may have been embarrassment over the 1978 award for stories in the Los Angeles *Times* on the lawsuit against Pacific Homes at the same time UMCom was doing public relations on this dispute.)

Candidates for the Stoody-West fellowship must be persons with a commitment to Christian communication, studying at an accredited university. The early awards were for study in journalism, but it has been broadened to include all areas of communication. It is not limited to United Methodists, and recipients have come from a number of denominations. Some have gone on to render outstanding service. The size of the award has risen with inflation and in 1981 it reached $6,000 a year.

Leonard M. Perryman was a dedicated staff member, respected and liked by all who knew him. Starting his newspaper career in Kansas City, Missouri, he worked for twelve years in the communication department of the Board of Global Ministries. He joined the news staff in 1967, working later in the Division of Program and Benevolence Interpretation. As a news writer he worked in New York and then Dayton. He was an associate editor of *The Interpreter* and directed promotion for several of the benevolence funds. He was a member of the staff team for the Periodical Publications Study of 1975, and he handled interpretation for the missional priority on the Ethnic Minority Local Church.

Perryman was a lifelong advocate for ethnic minority persons, and he was always keen for any measures to advance individuals. In 1983, while still on staff, he died of cancer. UMCom and his family determined to honor him with a scholarship for undergraduate study in communications by an ethnic minority person (Appendix D). The grant is $1,000 a year. As with the Stoody-West Fellowship, selections are made by a committee of the General Commission on Communication.

For a few years, beginning in 1962, TRAFCO awarded a Sockman Graduate Fellowship, honoring the Rev. Ralph W. Sockman, who preached every week on NBC radio for many years. It offered $3,500 a year for graduate study in theology or communication. One person who received the award (1964) was the Rev. David Abernathy, who subsequently was director of communications for the Southeastern Jurisdiction.

With the burgeoning complexity of communication methods and constant addition of new media, training for Christian communicators is a must. Hundreds of new persons must be trained every year. Those who already are at work must study to keep up to date.

Education for communication, in all its forms, is rising as a priority for UMCom. More can be expected in the years ahead.

·15·

Broad Horizons

Spring 1984. Amid the excitement of the Methodist bicentennial year, NBC Television airs an hour-long special on the contribution of women during 200 years of Methodism in America. Thousands of viewers experience this "Lost History."

October 1987. Editors of conference newspapers and other communicators gather in St. Louis to examine issues to come before the next year's General Conference.

These were major events for communications in The United Methodist Church, but United Methodist Communications could not have done them alone. The TV broadcast was arranged through the Communication Commission of the National Council of Churches. The pre-General Conference briefing was cosponsored with the United Methodist Association of Communicators.

These events illustrate the broad horizons that are characteristic of the UMCom outlook—an outlook that dates back fifty years to the agency's start.

Policy and practice join United Methodist Communications with co-workers within the denomination, both through formal arrangements and informal networks. Taking part in professional organizations helps staffers keep up to date. Ecumenical involvement broadens UMCom's effectiveness and makes a contribution in behalf of all United Methodists to a common Christian witness.

160

An Early Start

It began with the Rev. Ralph W. Stoody as he opened that first Methodist Information office in 1940. He quickly began forming in-church networks that later blossomed into the system of conference and area public relations offices and "national staff" gatherings to serve them. He joined professional societies to sharpen his skills, including the Public Relations Society of America and the Authors Guild. He worked with Religion in American Life. Through what was then the Department of Religious Radio of the Federal Council of Churches, he placed Methodists on network radio programs—a responsibility shortly turned over to the emerging TRAFCO.

TRAFCO used the channels of the Protestant Radio Commission and Protestant Film Commission as they combined into the Broadcasting and Film Commission, later the Communication Commission of the National Council of Churches of Christ in the U.S.A.

Within the church, TRAFCO worked with all agencies whenever they needed films produced. There was a special relationship with the then Methodist Publishing House and Board of Education because of the voluminous demand for teaching films in the church school curriculum. TRAFCO set up what it called its "consultative staff," made up of media specialists from the agencies. For years the group met twice a year to discuss productions, share information and learn about TRAFCO plans.

The Commission on Promotion and Cultivation built conference networks through its field staff. With the start of the program journal, an editorial council was formed so agencies could share in planning content of *The Methodist Story*. The commission was active in the Department of Stewardship and Benevolence (later Commission on Stewardship) of the NCCC.

The Evangelical United Brethren Church depended heavily on ecumenical agencies for audiovisual resources and radio-TV broadcasting. It too worked with the NCCC Communication Commission and the Commission on Stewardship.

A prominent ecumenist connected with communications was Charles C. Parlin, who was a member of the Commission on Public Relations and Methodist Information from the late 1950s to 1968. Traveling the world in ecumenical endeavors, he could be seen in far-away airports, scribbling postcards to boys in his Sunday school class at Englewood, New Jersey. For years he was active in the World Council of Churches, and in 1970 was elected as one of its presidents. He was one of the architects of Methodist-EUB union. He aided the press in many ways and helped communicators keep aware of the ecumenical dimension. Not least of his generous gestures were paying personally for the retirement banquet honoring Stoody and the press dinners at the opening of the WCC Assemblies in Evanston, 1954, and Uppsala, Sweden, 1968.

The broad horizons of the early years have continued to expand in United Methodist Communications. When predecessor agencies were combined into UMCom in 1972, all of the professional and ecumenical commitments were continued. New ventures ensued.

Internal Networks

Within the denomination, relationships between UMCom and the annual conferences are crucial. Much of this is informal, such as responding to inquiries or supplying speakers and workshop leaders. Conference communication staff often visit UMCom headquarters for consultation and training. Directors of conference media resource centers receive help as well.

Service to annual conferences is the purpose—reflected in its name—of the Office of Conference Services and Communication Education. It includes the field staff who work constantly with conference communicators. A newsletter, new in 1989, is called *Network*, symbolic of its purpose.

Care is taken that conference-level communicators are included in membership of the General Commission on Communication and consultative groups.

Among general agencies of the denomination UMCom has many ties. It could hardly function without them.

The Division of Production and Distribution has worked closely with the United Methodist Publishing House and the General Board of Discipleship in producing resources for the curriculum. The Division of Program and Benevolence Interpretation relates to each agency that receives support from general benevolences in order to tell the story of their work. United Methodist News Service covers the news of every church agency.

To provide a formal network and forum for communication concerns, UMCom sponsors a Communication Advisory Committee (CAC). Twice a year members of UMCom's staff and commission sit with representatives of general church agencies, jurisdictional fellowships, and conference communication offices. It is successor to the old TRAFCO Consultative Staff and what was begun in 1973 by the Joint Committee on Communications as the JCC Advisory Committee. The JCC Advisory Committee met immediately prior to JCC meetings and some confusion of roles resulted. Today's CAC is a place where persons doing communication work throughout the denomination can share information, co-ordinate planning and dream of the future.

The program journal's constant need for input from church agencies is served by what now is called Editorial Advisory Group for *The Interpreter*.

A network for United Methodist producers for radio and television began with a workshop in Nashville in 1990. Approximately eighty persons attended that gathering initiated by UMCom.

In the broad arena of co-operation among general agencies of the denomination, the UMCom general secretary meets regularly with the general secretaries of all agencies. And the UMCom general secretary and commission president hold seats on the General Council on Ministries.

Professional Organizations

Where can a person be certified as a professional communicator, win an award for a handsome brochure, and pick the brains of fellow-communicators for fresh ideas? The answer lies in the partnership between UMCom and the United Methodist Association of Communicators (UMAC).

The relationship goes back to what was once the Methodist Press Association, begun primarily for fellowship among editors of annual conference newspapers and general-church publications. For a long time it met in conjunction with annual meetings of the Board of Missions for a practical reason. The board had a policy of paying travel expense for editors of conference papers to come and, it was hoped, write about missions. Budget-strapped editors welcomed the free trip—and the chance to meet with the other editors. The Methodist Press Association counted staff of *The Methodist Story* among its members and, on occasion, officers.

The day came when church communications comprised much more than the sum of its publications. In 1973 the editors were joined by other communicators and the name became United Methodist Association of Communicators. First president was Sue Couch of the UMCom staff. Other staff persons have been actively involved and UMAC asks UMCom to designate one of its staff for liaison as a member of its executive committee. Today some two dozen of the UMCom staff are UMAC members, and they frequently win awards in UMAC competitions.

Through the years there have been significant joint projects between UMAC and UMCom. Among them are the certification program (Appendix E) and press briefings prior to the General Conference (Chapter 14). Established in 1983 was a Communicators' Hall of Fame (Appendix C). Each year a joint committee makes nominations from among United Methodist communicators who are retired or deceased. Awards are made at the UMAC annual meeting and the names are permanently displayed at UMCom headquarters and at the United Methodist Archives in Madison, New Jersey. By 1989, twenty-nine persons had been enshrined in the Hall of Fame.

Each of the five jurisdictions has a Fellowship of Communicators. Annual meetings offer friendships, idea exchange and continuing education. UMCom field staff encourage and assist the fellowships.

Professional associations beyond the denomination are important for UMCom staff for contacts and professional growth. Among those in which staff have held membership are the Public Relations Society of America, Society of Professional Journalists (formerly Sigma Delta Chi), Women in Communications, Inc. (formerly Theta Sigma Phi), Society of Motion Picture Technicians and Engineers, and National Academy of Television Arts and Sciences.

The Religious Public Relations Council has engaged a large number of UMCom staff. Founded in 1929 as Religious Publicity Council, it had among its charter members W. W. Reid and the Rev. Miron A. Morrill (Chapter 2). Also charter members were four other Methodists: (Miss) V. Ludel Boden and the Rev. Jay S. Stowell, Board of Home Missions and Church Extension; the Rev. Deets Pickett, Board of Temperance, Prohibition and Public Morals; and the Rev. Harry Earl Woolever, National Methodist Press; as well as L. B. Harnish, publicity secretary of the General Conference of the United Brethren in Christ.

United Methodists have been active both at the national and local levels. Thomas S. McAnally began a two-year hitch as national president in 1988. Among earlier presidents were Reid, 1931-33, Stowell, 1934-35 and 1936-38, the Rev. Ralph W. Stoody, 1945-46, the Rev. William C. Walzer, 1959-61, the Rev. David W. Gockley, 1964-66, Winston H. Taylor, 1967-69, and Sue Couch, 1979-80. Both Leonard Perryman and Robert Lear served as national treasurer.

Chapters of RPRC provide contacts and practical programs in cities where UMCom has offices. Staff have been active in those chapters, even in founding them. The Rev. Arthur West gave leadership in founding the chapter in Chicago and Edwin H. Maynard in Dayton. Among those serving as chapter presidents have been West, Maynard, the Rev. Earl K. Wood, Lear and Donald B. Moyer in Chicago; McAnally and the Rev. Ralph E. Baker in Nashville; Taylor, Roger L. Burgess, O. B. Fanning and Lear in Washington. Collier and Lear chaired committees for national RPRC conventions. In addition to UMCom staff, numbers of local and regional communicators have given chapter leadership.

165

Annual conventions of RPRC feature coveted awards, often won by UMCom. In 1978, for example, staff members received ten.

A parallel organization, with membership by publication, is the Associated Church Press (ACP), which serves church-related magazines and newspapers in the United States and Canada. Memberships are held by *The Interpreter* and *El Intérprete*. Maynard was president 1961-63; Darrell R. Shamblin served several terms as treasurer and board member, and Laura Okumu became a board member in 1990. Other United Methodists not on the UMCom staff have served in ACP, including the president elected in 1989, Mary Lou Redding of *The Upper Room*.

At the international level is the World Association for Christian Communication (WACC). The Rev. Harry C. Spencer was among the founders when, in 1972, two former organizations for Christian broadcasting and one for Christian literature were brought together. Dr. Spencer had been a founder of one of the predecessors, the World Association of Christian Broadcasters, and presided over its organizational meeting in Nairobi, Kenya, in 1963. He was asked to serve as acting general secretary of WACC for four months in 1973. The Rev. Curtis A. Chambers was secretary for several years. Elected president in 1988 was the Rev. William F. Fore, once a consultant for TRAFCO.

A regional unit is the North American Broadcast Section, commonly known as NABS/WACC. Staff in the Divisions of Public Media and Production and Distribution have been active, particularly in the annual meetings which showcase new productions and build networks.

Many of the organizations in which UMCom is involved join for a great decennial rally known as Religious Communication Congress. The first was in Chicago in 1970, the second in Nashville in 1980, and again in Nashville in 1990. Dr. Chambers was general chairperson for RCC 80.

Many of the UMCom staff were involved in hosting and providing programs for RCC 90. Dr. Burgess was on the planning committee and was executive producer for the convention's opening production and grand finale, which featured entertainer Steve Allen. J. Fred Rowles was producer for the multi-media opening gala involving four large-screen videos, bands on stage and in four corners of the room, singers, and television producer Bill Moyers as speaker. UMCom personnel helped staff the hospitality room and a display booth for the 1,300 participants, provided transportation for speakers, and gave behind-the-scenes support.

Ecumenical Enterprise

Other ecumenical endeavors are functional. They bring together communication units of several denominations to carry out certain projects, in contrast to those aimed at professional development.

One of the oldest of the functional units is now known as the Communication Commission of the National Council of the Churches of Christ in the U.S.A. It co-ordinates placement of programs on network television and of individuals on network shows. It is successor to the Broadcasting and Film Commission (BFC) and, before that, the Protestant Radio Commission and Protestant Film Commission. Spencer was one of the founders of BFC in 1950 and was chairman 1962-65. The change to Communication Commission came in 1973.

UMCom contributes from its budget to the Communication Commission and has several seats on its board, filled by staff and members of the General Commission on Communication. UMCom people have given leadership to the commission, taking their turns as officers. Serving terms as chair of BFC or the Communication Commission were Nelson Price, the Rev. Gene W. Carter and Chambers. Dr. Fore was for many years its chief executive.

Through this commission The United Methodist Church can place programming that networks would never accept from an individual denomination. United Methodists take their turn with other denominations in Christmas and Easter programs placed by the NCCC commission and in occasional specials.

The NCCC commission began in radio, but as television grew and radio went local, it has concentrated on the TV networks. Now UMCom works in radio with several other denominations through

167

SandCastles to produce and place Christian radio programs.

Originally serving the southern states, but increasingly national, is the Protestant Radio and Television Center in Atlanta. A major production is the *Protestant Hour* on radio. Preachers of the participating denominations are featured in rotation for 12-week segments. United Methodist participation is through the Joint Communications Commission of the Southeastern and South Central Jurisdictions and UMCom.

You see a billboard proclaiming: "Worship Together—Grow Together." You see the same message in buses and newspaper ads. You wonder how churches can advertise this way to encourage worship attendance. The answer is Religion in American Life (RIAL). It was formed in 1949 to work with the Advertising Council, through which the industry gives free advertising as a public service. More than forty religious groups are related to it. The interfaith board of RIAL determines annual themes, and an ad agency is assigned by the Advertising Council to create, produce and place the ads. RIAL seeks to support religious and moral values. Other recent themes, in addition to the one for 1984 quoted above, have been "Love Thy Family—Worship Together" and one on the Ten Commandments. In 1990 a ten-year attendance campaign began with the theme "Invite a friend to your house."

In its early years Stoody was active in RIAL, and UMCom has had continuous representation on its board. For more than fifteen years United Methodist Dr. Gockley was president of RIAL. Current board members in 1990 include Burgess and Bishop Rueben P. Job.

A significant instrument for research into the effects of television and the creation of tools to deal with the situations discovered is the Media Action Research Center (MARC). It was begun in 1974 with $45,000 of seed money from UMCom. Price was one of the founders, working with Dr. Robert M. Liebert of the State University of New York at Stony Brook, a psychologist and research specialist. Price was first president of MARC (and as of 1990 its only president). The first secretary-treasurer was Ben. T. Logan of UMCom's Public Media staff, who continued until 1989.

Work done by MARC has included research into the effects of

television on viewers, especially children; studies of violence on television; and studies of stereotyping of women and ethnic minorities in TV programming. A significant product was the children's television spots (Chapter 10), intended to insert positive values into children's programming. MARC also conducted Television Awareness Training (Chapter 14).

Another endeavor that now represents six denominations, the National Council of Churches, the World Council of Churches, and a Roman Catholic Order, is EcuFilm (Chapter 11). Operated by UMCom, it rents and sells the film and video resources of the co-operative members.

Newest venture is the Vision Interfaith Satellite Network (VISN), which feeds eighteen hours a day of religious programming to cable television networks. Price and Wilford V. Bane were among those who shared the dream for this way to distribute religious programs, and they helped put together a broad-based coalition to make it happen. The twenty-two members represent faith traditions as diverse as Salvation Army, African Methodist Episcopal, Mormon, Jewish and Greek Orthodox. Bane served nearly two years as general manager while on loan from the UMCom staff. Price became president and chief executive officer in 1990. VISN carries the *Catch the Spirit* series and other programs produced by UMCom.

In addition to the NCCC Communication Commission, UMCom co-operates with other departments of the National Council of the Churches of Christ in the U.S.A. Staff have served on the supervisory committee for the Office of Information, which handles public relations for the NCCC. Staff have participated also in Intermedia, which represents the NCCC in communication ministries overseas. (Spencer had been a founder of RAVEMCO, an organization to encourage use of audiovisuals overseas; RAVEMCO joined with Lit-Lit, a literacy and literature agency, to form Intermedia.) The Division of Program and Benevolence Interpretation continues a long-time interest in the Commission on Stewardship.

From time to time UMCom staff have been involved in committees and special programs of the World Council of

Churches, including its Christian Literature Fund. Lear spent four months in Geneva in 1968 on loan to the WCC Office of Communication. At WCC General Assemblies, once every six or seven years, UMCom's News Service supplies one or more persons for the news room. UMCom also contributes staff for news operations when the WCC holds a major meeting in the United States.

The UMNS staff operates the news room for the World Methodist Conference whenever and wherever it meets.

One other arena of ecumenical cooperation is the Consultation on Church Union (COCU), in which from eight to ten (at various times) denominations explore ways to move toward union. News Service helps with press relations for major COCU events. Lear served for a year as acting press officer in addition to his News Service duties.

Exchange of staff is also a means of ecumenical co-operation. This is done mainly by News Service, and the most frequent partner has been the Christian Church (Disciples of Christ). United Methodist staff have helped in the news room at Disciples General Assemblies, and Disciples have helped at United Methodist General Conferences.

Proud as it is of its multiple ecumenical involvements, UMCom never forgets its primary obligation to The United Methodist Church. It is proud of the United Methodist heritage and devotes most of its energies to serving the church.

But just as The United Methodist Church has an ecumenical commitment, so UMCom has its ecumenical commitment. Communication in that context spreads the United Methodist message more widely and makes a profound statement of Christian unity.

And the chances are that UMCom's ecumenical horizon will grow even wider in the future.

·16·

Into the Future

*I*t's going to be different!

That is the surest forecast one can make about communications in the year 2040. We know that change will continue—and will accelerate. We can only speculate as to how well the church will manage to make use of new media—and there surely will be some—or of the old media, revised and improved.

Prediction has always been a risky business, but not always as difficult as it is now. Picture yourself in 1890, anticipating how the church might be communicating in 1940.

You would have thought almost entirely in terms of print. You would have thought of the church publications flourishing in that day—*The Religious Telescope*, *The Messenger*, a handful of *Christian Advocates*, and several papers in German. You might have predicted bright futures for them, with a growing population, growing church membership and increased circulations. You would have been partly right, except that by 1940 the Great Depression had shriveled some circulations and forced mergers. And most of the church papers in German were a memory.

For communicating with its own members, the church in 1940 was about like the church of 1890. It relied on newspapers, supplemented by some magazines and of course book publishing. The prognosticator of 1890 certainly would have been aware of the daily newspapers, but it might not have occurred to him/her that

171

the giant step of 1940 would be a systematic effort to get news of the church into the public press.

And the forecaster of 1890 would scarcely have imagined that the day's experiments with "wireless telegraphy" would have blossomed into radio and an entirely new way of communicating. And a new opportunity for the church.

Forecast the Revolution?

So, the 1890 forecaster would have been mainly right, though probably missing at some important points. But that was easy compared to the person in 1940 forecasting 1990.

Certainly those at the General Conference of 1940 who asked for "an intelligent church" would never have dreamed that the modest bureau they set up would have become a major communication force, using a professional staff with a dozen different specialties, employing 125 or more persons and spending more than $12 million a year.

Even less likely would they have dreamed that the communication agency they began would be telling the church's story by colored motion pictures in a box and getting those pictures from here to there by bouncing electronic signals off a human-made satellite.

Press relations, the concern of the 1940 General Conference, still plays a major role in the work of United Methodist Communications. But most of the other activities described in the chapters of this book were scarcely imagined then.

The planners of 1940 did not know that a revolution in how people communicate was even then beginning. They did not realize that the church would have to strain to keep up with that revolution.

The story of these fifty years has been the story of the revolution: demanding, frustrating, promising, expensive—and rewarding beyond anyone's dream. It has been the story of the church's response to enlarging media opportunities. It has been a response slowed at times by traditional thinking and always by a shortage of funds. But it has also been a response with many victories and exciting prospects for the future as UMCom continues to help the church tell its story.

Forecasts for 2040

But if people of 1940 could not imagine what church communications of 1990 would be like, what can we say about 2040?

Ignoring the peril, we have asked a dozen informed church persons to venture their guess about the next fifty years.

They are agreed on one thing: it's going to be different. Everyone acknowledges the certainty of change, and the ever-faster speed of change. They are confident the church will be doing its best to take advantage of the media opportunities of 2040, but as to what that will look like . . . well, each has his or her own idea.

"Interactive audio/video technology will permit instant access to individuals and events throughout the world (and beyond) and to the accumulated wisdom of the ages. The church's fundamental task, however, will remain unchanged: to seek and speak the truth, lest each succeeding generation know more but understand less than its predecessors."

—Harry Johnson, manager of corporate communications, Polaroid Corporation, and commission member, 1972-80

"By the year 2040 we will be communicating—as we have already begun to—by computer and satellite. The television set will have become obsolete; we will enjoy 'laserviewers' which will vastly improve sound and picture quality. The local church member will return to the forefront of the church as a result of a nationwide, and possibly global, integrated computer system affordable to all. This will greatly improve the connectiveness of our church. The church is now behind technologically and in order for our church to be good—no, *great*—communicators with the unchurched and with each other, we will have to reorganize some of our priorities."

—Cynthia Abrams, communications chairperson of the Native American International Caucus; a recent journalism graduate

"People will be doing shopping, banking and most everything else by push-phones. The field of communication is going to make life so much more impersonal that the church will have a very large, important need to fill for the inter-personal. I think the church will be pretty slow to be highly technological. We probably will not forsake the sermon."
—Barbara Blackstone, Department of Communication, Slippery Rock University of Pennsylvania; commission member 1976-84

"By 2040 The United Methodist Church should be in every household every day with the message of the gospel. I see the possibility of frequent and brief messages from the church to the listening audience with an opportunity for instant response. By 2040 television will be much more interactive and the viewers will be able to respond quickly to a message, question or offer. What if every addictive person, every lonely person, every ill person, every homebound person, every hospitalized person, could see and hear the gospel through modern communication technology and could respond in such a way that human resources could be quickly dispatched to those persons?"
—Bishop Rueben P. Job, president, General Commission on Communication, 1988-92

"Technological developments will be wonderful: a universal audio-video-computer plug to connect anyone to anyone, anywhere; 3-D hologram TV; computers that talk, listen and think. But the social consequences will be terrifying: a few huge corporations will control the media. Ten years ago it was fifty; today it is twenty-nine; in fifty years it may be three. Multinationals will dominate the world economy, nation-states and all cultures—because they will dominate the media. Communication will be used for control more than ever: more bread (fast-food) and circuses (holographic TV) for the masses; less real diversity and individualism."
—William F. Fore, communication professor at Yale Divinity School; president of the World Association for Christian Communication

"Although the technology will change, it will be the communication of the individual's personal experience of Jesus

174

Christ in his or her life that will enable others to know the love offered by God. As our church is whittled down to the faithful few, God will enable those of us who have the joy that comes from knowing God to make more and more breakthroughs with innovative uses of media to communicate the love expressed by Jesus Christ. This will happen as those in the faith use the language of the times—whatever that language may be and in whatever context of community—to communicate the story of God's love and faithfulness to us."
—Lynn S. Clark, 1988 winner of the Stoody-West Fellowship; a seminary staff person moonlighting as video writer/producer

"Cable television will continue to grow, with a serious shakeout of small networks by the year 2000. Teleconferencing will become a way of life. Computer networks will expand. Large organizations like The United Methodist Church will become electronic networks so financial and other data can be passed back and forth. This may lead to a new kind of curriculum publishing. With high-speed laser printers, local churches can print off their own copies from a central computer with color and illustrations. A central ordering system for United Methodist resources will become a reality. Advertising and public relations will no longer be dirty words for mainline churches."
—Roger L. Burgess, general secretary, United Methodist Communications

"The future media terrain will feature life which is both radically different and very much the same. Huge technological and social shifts will flood every person's life. The present churches' non-efficient buildings, awesome hierarchies dedicated to clergy, and irrelevant worship and programming will serve only a few or disappear entirely. A new Christian spirituality will replace today's denominational religion. The intermix of omnipresent media, isolated individuals, and convulsing society will be transformed into fresh faith expressions by Jesus Christ for the age."
—Dennis C. Benson, director of the graduate program in religious communication, United Theological Seminary

"The year 2040 should not be led by the technological advances,

175

but rather by the need for expanding messengers of the Gospel. While technology races ahead, the people of the world are demanding a voice and a means of getting that voice around the globe. In the United States, the majority population will be people of color with varying cultures and languages. The church's leadership role is to be a model for inclusive, healing and culturally relevant communication."
—Sharon Maeda, president, Spectra Communications, Inc.; commission member 1981-88

"When I think of the future I think of picture phones, computer networking and group communications—like closed circuit satellite meetings so we can go to our offices and meet with people in five different places and nobody has to leave town. But there are some things that are here to stay—like print. But printed communications will change. The 'sound bite' approach of *USA Today* is going to creep over into all kinds of communications. I hope the church will use high tech in the future more than it has in the past."
—Mary Lou Redding, an editor of *The Upper Room* and president, the Associated Church Press

"For me the future of Christian communication is more a question. Will church communication in 2040 be characterized by truthfulness and integrity so that the gospel is believed and acted upon? Or, will it be like the slick advertising that sells to consumers? The technologies that are used will not matter as much as the authenticity of what is communicated."
—David W. Briddell, director of Intermedia, National Council of Churches

"Can you imagine a church without walls? The church as the communion of all believers will be a reality. Electronics will take you to meetings and even the worship service will be an ethereal experience. You'll sit in your living room with your family surrounded by other worshippers brought to you via 3-D television."
—Julio Gómez, pastor; member of La Junta Consultiva de Comunicaciones

Choices of the Future

So the revolution continues. Our panel expects change, with media opportunities we cannot imagine. They foresee that the sophistication of communication techniques will increase, and the costs increase in proportion. Even as in the past fifty years, the church of the future will face agonizing choices as to how to invest wisely its resources for communication.

We of 1990 cannot make those choices. They belong to the next generation. But we can send this word of advice to the future: The church must constantly renew its commitment to communication. Just as Jesus and the apostles used the media of their day—storytelling and writing on papyrus—so the church in any age must use the media available to it.

Our 1990 words of advice to communicators of the future might well be these, from the UMCom Mission Statement:

SHARE Christ's message with the church and the world.

LISTEN to the needs of the church and the world.

INTERPRET the general program of the church to United Methodist members.

PROMOTE giving to World Service and other general funds of the church.

CREATE communication systems and print, electronic and audiovisual resources.

MARKET communication resources to United Methodists, the wider Christian community and the general public.

OUR MISSION is to help the church tell its story.

Appendices

Presiding Officers and Chief Executive Officers

The Methodist Church

Commission on Public Information, 1940-52; Commission on Public Relations and Methodist Information, 1952-68
Presiding Officer (Chairman, 1940-56; President, 1956-68)
    G. Bromley Oxnam, 1940-48
    Richard C. Raines, 1948-60
    Eugene M. Frank, 1960-68
Chief Executive Officer (Director, 1940-48; Executive Director, 1948-56; General Secretary, 1956-68)
    Ralph W. Stoody, 1940-64
    Arthur West, 1964-68

Radio and Film Commission, 1948-56; Television, Radio and Film Commission, 1956-68
Presiding Officer (Chairman, 1948-52; President, 1952-68)
    Donald H. Tippett, 1948-64
    Aubrey G. Walton, 1964-68
Chief Executive Officer (Chairman of the Joint Staff, 1948-52; Executive Secretary, 1952-56; General Secretary, 1956-68)
    Howard E. Tower, 1948-52
    Harry C. Spencer, 1952-68

Commission on Promotion and Cultivation, 1952-68
Presiding Officer (President, 1952-68)
    William C. Martin, 1952-64
    Donald H. Tippett, 1964-68

178

Chief Executive Officer (Executive Director, 1952-56; General Secretary, 1956-68)
    E. Harold Mohn, 1952-60
    Elliott L. Fisher, 1960-65
    Howard Greenwalt, 1965-68

The Evangelical United Brethren Church

Committee on Communication, 1960-62; Department of Communication, 1962-68 (both within the Council of Administration)
Presiding Officer (Chairman of the Department Committee, 1962-68)
    Donald R. Lantz, 1962-68
Chief Executive Officer (Director of the Department, 1962-68)
    Paul V. Church, 1962-68
NOTE: Dr. Church was also general secretary of the Council of Administration. He formed the Committee on Communication about 1960, and the 1962 General Conference authorized the Department of Communication with a governing committee. Staff was loaned by program agencies.

The United Methodist Church

Commission on Public Relations and (United) Methodist Information, 1968-72
Presiding Officer (Chairman, 1968-72)
    Eugene M. Frank, 1968-72
Chief Executive Officer (Executive Secretary, 1968-72)
    Arthur West, 1968-72

Division of Television, Radio and Film Communication (Division of the Program Council), 1968-72
Presiding Officer (Chairman, 1968-72)
    Aubrey G. Walton, 1968-72
Chief Executive Officer (Associate General Secretary, 1968-72)
    Harry C. Spencer, 1968-72

Division of Interpretation (Division of the Program Council), 1968-72
Presiding Officer (Chairman, 1968-72)
    R. Marvin Stuart, 1968-72
Chief Executive Officer (Associate General Secretary, 1968-72)
    Howard Greenwalt, 1968-72

United Methodist Communications: Joint Committee on Communications, 1972-80; General Commission on Communication, 1980-
Presiding Officer (President, 1972-   )
    Thomas P. Moore, 1972-76
    Charles J. Cappleman, 1976-84
    Louis W. Schowengerdt, 1984-88
    Rueben P. Job, 1988-
Chief Executive Officer (Executive Secretary, 1972-76; General Secretary, 1976-   )
    Paul V. Church (acting), 1972-73
    Curtis A. Chambers, 1973-84
    Roger L. Burgess, 1984-

APPENDIX B

Milestones

A Chronology of Major Events in the Life of UMCom

1939—Union of three denominations forms The Methodist Church.

1940—Methodist General Conference authorizes a public information agency. Ralph Stoody opens office in New York.

1941—Methodist Information has offices in New York, Nashville and Chicago.

1944—A professional staff of three provides press services for General Conference. Beginning of the Crusade for Christ, an ancestor of the Commission on Promotion and Cultivation. First District Superintendents' Convocation held. Methodist Information names a "representative to the Negro press."

1946—Union of two denominations forms the Evangelical United Brethren Church.

1948—A Radio and Film Commission is formed by Methodists with no budget or staff. Advance for Christ and His Church, a four-year program, brings Harold Mohn into promotional work.

1949—First area public relations office established in Indiana.

1950—First publication of Luccock book, *Endless Line of Splendor* (reissued in 1964 and 1975).

1952—Extensive radio and television coverage of General Conference. Radio and Film Commission reauthorized, now with staff and budget, Harry Spencer executive secretary and office in Nashville. Commission on Promotion and Cultivation authorized, Mohn is executive director, office in Chicago.

1953—Stoody provides public relations for Bishop Oxnam at congressional hearing. Film on John Wesley is released. First National News Consultation is held.

1954—Weekly news summary, *Methodists Make News*, begins.

1955—*Spotlight* begins as program journal for the EUB Church.

1956—"Television" added to name of Television, Radio and Film Commission; calls itself TRAFCO. Methodist Information opens Washington office. Program journal, *The Methodist Story*, is established.

1958—Spanish-language program journal, later named *El Intérprete*, begins.

1959—Three members of TRAFCO staff lose lives in airline crash. Distribution of World Service leaflets nears three million.

1960—Elliott Fisher heads Commission on Promotion and Cultivation.

180

1962—Department of Communication formed within EUB Council of Administration.

1963—TRAFCO opens New York and Hollywood offices.

1964—Arthur West directs Methodist Information. Stoody Fellowship is established (in 1981 Stoody-West Fellowship). Conference on "The Church in the Communications Revolution" sponsored by TRAFCO.

1965—Howard Greenwalt is general secretary of Commission on Promotion and Cultivation.

1966—*Night Call* radio program begins (revived in 1968).

1968—The United Methodist Church is formed. Cross and Flame insigne created by Division of Interpretation. TRAFCO and promotional agency become divisions of the Program Council.

1969—Combined program journal takes name, *The Interpreter*.

1972—United Methodist Communications (UMCom) formed by combining United Methodist Information, TRAFCO and the Division of Interpretation. Arthur West, Spencer and Greenwalt head three new divisions of UMCom.

1973—Curtis Chambers becomes general secretary of UMCom; headquarters in Dayton. James Campbell heads Division of Production and Distribution. Funds promoted by Division of Program and Benevolence Interpretation call for $60 million a year.

1974—UMCom plays leading role in establishing Media Action Research Center; Nelson Price is president. (MARC later sponsors Television Awareness Training.)

1975—InfoServ and United Methodist Film Service (later EcuFilm) are established. Price heads Public Media Division. Study of church periodicals calls for a Comprehensive Communication System.

1977—Readus Watkins heads Division of Program and Benevolence Interpretation. Central news desk set up by News Service. *Connection* radio program begins (continuing until 1981).

1978—UMCom President Charles Cappleman proposes a strong movement into television, including purchase of a TV station. UMCom collaborates with caucus in planning first Asian-American Convocation. Assistance begins for *Now*, United Methodist Black newspaper.

1979—Peggy West heads Division of Production and Distribution.

1980—General Conference authorizes raising $25 million outside normal benevolences for television. Campaign fails in 1981.

1981—New office/studio building opens in Nashville; cost of $2.2 million for 34,000 square feet. Public relations office for denomination opens. UMCom helps Native American International Caucus establish newspaper, *Echo of the Four Winds*.

181

1983—CircuitWriter computer network begins. News Service gathers and distributes news by computer.

1984—Roger Burgess becomes general secretary of UMCom; headquarters are moved to Nashville. UMCom helps celebration of 200th anniversary of Methodism in America. Television/Telecommunication Fund set up by General Conference. Satellite teleconferencing and video link four scattered locations in an educational seminar.

1985—*Catch the Spirit*, half-hour weekly TV program, begins. Donald Collier heads Division of Program and Benevolence Interpretation.

1986—With building addition, staff is consolidated in Nashville except for continuing Public Media offices in New York and Washington, plus regionally deployed field staff.

1988—TV/T Fund blanketed into World Service for continued funding of television and telecommunications. Twenty-two denominations begin distributing television programs via Vision Interfaith Satellite Network.

1989—Plans begin for a program journal in the Korean language. First live uplink to satellite from UMCom studio.

1990—Fiftieth anniversary of establishment of a communication agency for what is now The United Methodist Church.

APPENDIX C

Communicators' Hall of Fame

The Communicators' Hall of Fame is maintained by the United Methodist Association of Communicators with co-operation by UMCom. The names of persons inducted into the Hall of Fame are enshrined in the UMCom building in Nashville, and the United Methodist Archives in Madison, New Jersey. The Hall of Fame began in 1983 and recognizes persons who are retired and have rendered distinguished service in communications at the local, annual conference, jurisdictional or general church level for at least ten years.

The names of persons enshrined are listed here, identified by their major career responsibilities.

1983
Arthur West, head of Methodist Information and UMCom Public Media Division.
Harry C. Spencer, head of TRAFCO and UMCom Division of Production and Distribution.

Walter N. Vernon, Jr., writer, historian, editor of church-school materials and secretary of TRAFCO.

T. Otto Nall, editor of *Christian Advocate*, bishop.

Nolan B. Harmon, book editor for the church, bishop.

B. F. Jackson, pioneer in use of audiovisuals, writer.

Prince A. Taylor, Jr., editor of *Central Christian Advocate*, bishop.

Dorothy McConnell, editor of *The Methodist Woman*.

Robert Sands, editor and public relations director in Illinois and Iowa (posthumous award).

1984

Wesley Brashares, pioneer in area public relations, commission member for TRAFCO.

L. Scott Allen, editor of *Central Christian Advocate*, bishop.

Joe Willard Krecker, editor of *Telescope-Messenger*.

Mary McLanahan, editor of *World Evangel*.

Leonard M. Perryman, news writer for the Board of Missions and Methodist Information and for UMCom, an editor for *The Interpreter* (posthumous award).

1985

Raymond M. Veh, editor of *Builders*.

O. B. Fanning, a news director for Methodist Information.

Rowena Ferguson, editor of Christian education materials, author.

Ann Ashmore, conference newspaper editor in Mississippi.

Ralph W. Stoody, director and general secretary of Methodist Information (posthumous award).

1986

Newman S. Cryer, editor of *Methodist Layman*, staff of *New Christian Advocate*, and public relations director in Indiana.

Woodrow A. Geier, editor of *The Pastor* and publications in Christian education.

Harold H. Hazenfield, editor of EUB adult publications and editor of program materials for UMCom.

Roland E. Wolseley, journalist, author, and director of religious journalism studies at Syracuse University.

Daniel L. Ridout, news writer and editor for the Central Jurisdiction and Methodist Information (posthumous award).

1987

Carl E. Keightley, editor of the *Texas Methodist*.

T. C. Whitehouse, writer, editor of *Zion's Herald*.

Ewing T. Wayland, editor of *Arkansas Methodist*, *Louisiana Methodist* and *Together*.

Betty Marchant, audiovisual specialist for the Board of Global Ministries.

William Watkins Reid, director of news service for the Board of Missions (posthumous award).

1988
Arthur Moore, Jr., editor of *World Outlook.*
Frances Smith, ecumenical writer and reporter, news director for UMCom.
A. McKay Brabham, Jr., editor of *South Carolina Methodist Advocate.*
John Young, area and conference director of communications in Ohio.
Robert F. Storey, West Ohio Conference director of communications
  (posthumous award).
Toge Fujihira, photographer and cinematographer for the Board of Missions
  (posthumous award).

1989
Georgia M. Daily, editor of *Arkansas United Methodist.*
William M. Holt, editor of *Wesleyan Christian Advocate.*
Floyd A. Johnson, artist for *Together* magazine.
Edwin H. Maynard, editor/editorial director of *The Methodist Story* and *The
  Interpreter,* administrator for UMCom.
Lewis O. Hartman, editor of *Zions Herald,* bishop.

APPENDIX D

Fellowship and Scholarship Winners

Stoody-West Fellowship

Established in 1964, the fellowship first honored the Rev. Ralph W. Stoody,
director and general secretary of Methodist Information from 1940 until his
retirement in 1964. In 1981 the name was changed to "Stoody-West" in honor
of the Rev. Arthur West, who led the agency from 1964 until his retirement in
1975 as head of the Public Media Division of UMCom. The fellowship awards a
monetary grant for graduate study in journalism by a person already engaged in
religious journalism or planning to enter the field. The purpose is "to enhance
the recipient's professional competence and thereby to help perpetuate the
standards exemplified by Dr. Stoody and Dr. West."

1965-66	Robert C. Welling, West Virginia University
1966-67	Victoria G. Benson, Syracuse University
1967-68	Katherine P. Satrom, Northwestern University
1968-69	Ronald P. Patterson, Syracuse University
1969-70	George M. Daniels, Columbia University
1970-71	Happy James Lawrence, University of Tennessee
1971-72	Marian S. Crooks, Ohio University (Athens)

1972-73 No award
1973-74 Mark R. Day, University of Southern California
1974-75 Patricia Diane Weddington, Duke University
1975-76 Myra Davis, North Carolina A & T State University
1976-77 Lawrence S. Ayo Ladigbolu, Southern Methodist University
1977-78 Jan Lichtenwalter, Ohio State University
1978-79 Donald D. Cowan, Northwestern University
1979-80 Gladys Ophelia Wilson-Beach, New York University
1980-81 William L. Dockery, University of Tennessee
1981-82 Ann B. Jones, Boston University
1982-83 Denise R. Johnson-Stovall, Northwestern University
1983-84 Debra Joy Hostetler, Indiana University
1984-85 Leah Gallardo, California State University in Los Angeles
1985-86 John Paul Godges, Georgetown University
1986-87 Grace Poore, Syracuse University
1987-88 Debra Rhey Hockanson, University of Missouri, Columbia
1988-89 Lynn S. Clark, United Theological Seminary (half year)
         Cynthia B. Hopson, Murray (Ky.) State University (half year)
1989-90 Christian Nuckols, Northwestern University
1990-91 Larry Ramey, United Theological Seminary

Perryman Scholarship

The Leonard M. Perryman Communications Scholarship for Ethnic Minority Students honors Mr. Perryman, a journalist serving the church for nearly thirty years in the Board of Missions and United Methodist Communications. At the time of his death in 1983 he was a reporter for United Methodist News Service and associate editor of *The Interpreter*. The scholarship is for undergraduate study (junior or senior year) for an ethnic minority person who intends to pursue a career in religious communication. The scholarship was first offered in 1988.

1988-89 Kelli Kirkpatrick, Columbia College (Chicago)
1989-90 Dennis Galolo, University of Hawaii
1990-91 Celeste Ryan, Columbia Union College

APPENDIX E

Certification in Christian Communication

The certification program was begun in 1979 as a joint project of the United Methodist Association of Communicators and UMCom. The purpose is to provide accreditation as peer recognition and to meet a requirement for diaconal ministry. Candidates must meet standards established by the two sponsors. Certification is for four years, subject to renewal at four-year intervals. The supervising committee represents both UMAC and UMCom. (Dates following certain names indicate renewals.)

1980
J. Frederick Rowles, 1984, 1988
Ruth Ward Laughlin, 1984, 1988
Earl Kenneth Wood
Nell Matthews, 1984, 1988
Winston H. Taylor, 1984, 1988
Edwin H. Maynard, 1984, 1988
Gwen Christensen, 1984, 1988
Florence L. Williams
Sue Siebert, 1984, 1988
Marvin D. James
John T. Wylie, 1984, 1988
Robert F. Storey, 1984
G. Roy Lawrence
Philip D. Hill, 1984, 1988

1981
Geraldine L. Hodson, 1985
Barbara J. Wilkinson, 1985
John A. Lovelace, 1985
Mary Brooke Casad, 1985
Charles K. Biedka
Timothy E. Coppock
Bette Prestwood, 1985, 1990
John L. Borchert, 1985
Kris M. Wilhelmi, 1985
Leonard M. Perryman

1982
Ronald C. Melzer, 1986
Joan Gray LaBarr, 1986
Kenneth Brown, 1986
Clyde W. Chesnutt
Mearle Griffith, 1986
Raymond L. Wiblin

1983
Sharon L. Blackwell, 1987
Bettie W. Story, 1987
Elizabeth Glidden, 1987
Roderick Hargo, 1987
Garlinda Burton, 1988
Carolyn Simms, 1987

1984
Reinhard Brose
Paul E. Ruark
James H. Steele, 1988
Keith A. Muhleman, 1988
Kim Rose
Elwood Fleming
Katherine Kruger Noble, 1988
Kenneth Horn, 1988
Finees Flores
Newtonia Harris Coleman, 1988

1985
No candidates certified

1986
No candidates certified

1987
Kay C. Burns
Cyndy Schillinger
Dana M. Bunn

1988
Joseph C. Beavon
Diana L. Bertholf
Boyce A. Bowdon
Mary Lou Krause
Julianne McAchran
Dulci McCoy
Geneva Morrison
Jean Noren
Roger L. Burgess
Donnalee Sanderson

1989
Dana E. Jones
James R. Woodrick
Shirley W. Struchen
Lillian Sills

1990
Marilyn Kasperek

APPENDIX F

Members of the General Commission on Communication 1989-92

From the Council of Bishops

Rueben P. Job (President)
L. Bevel Jones III
Richard B. Wilke

From the North Central Jurisdiction

James E. Magaw
Robert E. Ball
Florence Woods
Dorothy Schmidt

From the Northeastern Jurisdiction

G. Edwin Zeiders
Blair A. Gilbert
Joan G. Nagle
Patricia Bigler

From the South Central Jurisdiction

James W. Moore
Russell Coker, Jr.
Mary Silva (Vice-President)
Sammie Ellis Rainey

From the Southeastern Jurisdiction

Charles L. Johnson
Warren P. Kynard
Barbara Wilcox
Richard B. Faris

From the Western Jurisdiction

Lane C. Rees
Christine Kemp
Sherylan Gay Thorson
Kristin K. Knudson

From the General Council on Ministries

George R. DuVall
Helen H. Slentz

Additional Members

Helen K. Chang
Wendy Reid Crisp
G. Alan Dunlap
Richard Eldredge
Ron Hull
Stephen S. Kim
Joan Gray LaBarr
James W. Lane (Secretary)
John Lovelace
J. LaVonne Moore
Robert W. Norvet
W. Mearl Purvis
Lenora C. Stephens
George A. Tanner
Carlos Verdecia

APPENDIX G

Theological Understandings That Guide Our Work

Communicating the Good News of God's transforming grace and reconciliation of the world through Christ is the mission of the Church. This communication of the Gospel is made real by the work of the Holy Spirit.

In the prologue to John's Gospel, the creative and redemptive self-expression of God is described as the "Word." God's Word addresses us in the created universe, in the history of the covenant people of God and through the incarnation. The scriptures and the Church bear witness to this revelation through the inspiration of the Holy Spirit.

Through the Holy Spirit, God is continuously freeing us to respond to the divine call and empowering us to express ourselves. In Jesus we see the fullness of human freedom and expression as well as the fullness of God's presence. As Jesus' disciples and friends, we, too, express our freedom through the communication of God's Word.

Therefore, The United Methodist Church rejoices in its opportunity to communicate the good news of Christ Jesus to persons within and outside the church. The United Methodist Church calls everyone to awareness of and encourages commitment to Jesus as the Christ. In response to God's call, the Church proclaims the Gospel message by using the many means of communication that God has made available to us: preaching, witness, service, print, audiovisuals, and electronic media.

Communication is among people. We hear as well as speak. Good communication requires listening. The Church must listen with Christian hearts to the voices of the world.

The responsibility for communication belongs to each church member, pastor, congregation, institution, board and agency of the Church. Within this total responsibility, the General Conference has assigned certain functions to the General Commission on Communication. These functions include providing leadership in witness through every available communication channel.

Adopted April 1975
Revised October 1987

Bibliography

Official Records

The Book of Discipline and comparable books of discipline by various names for The United Methodist Church, The Methodist Church, the Evangelical United Brethren Church, the Methodist Episcopal Church, and the Methodist Episcopal Church, South. Various years.

Journals of General Conferences of The United Methodist Church, The Methodist Church, the Evangelical United Brethren Church and the Methodist Protestant Church. Various years.

Reports to General Conferences, particularly the *Blue Book of Reports* (EUB), *Quadrennial Reports* (Methodist) and report pages of the advance editions of the *Daily Christian Advocate* (United Methodist). Various years.

Daily Christian Advocate (proceedings) of General Conference of The Methodist Church and The United Methodist Church, 1939-1988.

General Minutes of the Annual Conferences, The Methodist Church and The United Methodist Church. Various years.

Annual Reports of United Methodist Communications, TRAFCO, Methodist Information, and Commission on Promotion and Cultivation. Various years.

Minutes of the governing commissions and committees of UMCom and predecessor agencies. Various dates.

Books

Behney, J. Bruce, and Paul H. Eller, *The History of the Evangelical United Brethren Church*. Nashville, Abingdon Press, 1979.

189

Bucke, Emory S., general editor, *The History of American Methodism*, 3 vols. New York and Nashville, Abingdon Press, 1964.

Cornish, Edward, editor, *Communications Tomorrow: The Coming of the Information Society.* Bethesda, Md., World Future Society, 1983.

Davis, Lyman Edwyn, *Democratic Methodism in America.* New York, Fleming H. Revell, 1921.

Dugan, George, Casper H. Nannes and R. Marshall Stross, *RPRC: A 50-Year Reflection.* New York, Religious Public Relations Council, 1979.

Eller, Paul H., *These Evangelical United Brethren.* Dayton, Otterbein Press, 1957.

Fore, William F., *Broadcasting and The Methodist Church 1952-1972*, doctoral dissertation. Ann Arbor, University Microfilms.

Gilbert, George, *Photography: The Early Years.* New York, Harper & Row, 1980.

Goodspeed, Edgar J., *Christianity Goes to Press.* New York, MacMillan, 1940.

Maddox, Brenda, *Beyond Babel: New Directions in Communications.* New York, Simon & Schuster, 1972.

Ness, John H., Jr., *One Hundred Fifty Years.* Dayton, Board of Publication of the EUB Church, 1966.

Pilkington, James Penn, *The Methodist Publishing House: A History*, Vol. 1. Nashville, Abingdon Press, 1968.

Stoody, Ralph W., *A Handbook of Church Public Relations.* New York and Nashville, Abingdon Press, 1959.

Other Publications and Sources

Program Journals: *Spotlight*, 1955-72; *The Methodist Story*, 1957-72; *Methodist Story-Spotlight*, 1972; *The Interpreter*, 1973-89.

Newsletters: *Mine, Share* and *Sharing*, Methodist Information, to 1973; *Continuity*, TRAFCO, 1956-73; *Sharing-Continuity*, UMCom, 1973-77; *UMCommunicator*, UMCom, 1977-84; *Network*, UMCom, 1989-

Transcripts from UMCom Oral History Project.

UMCom papers deposited in the United Methodist Archives, Madison, New Jersey.

Index

Index

196

About the Author

Edwin H. Maynard wrote this history and, at times, also carried many of the responsibilities described herein. He began his career in religious journalism in 1946 on the news staff of the *Christian Advocate*, having worked before World War II on two secular publications.

In 1956 he was recruited from *Together*, Methodism's family magazine, to be the first editor of *The Methodist Story*, a denominational program journal. He became editorial director of the Commission on Promotion and Cultivation of The Methodist Church in 1964 and continued writing and editing in that office through church union until 1977, when he became assistant general secretary of United Methodist Communications.

Known for his high energy level and prodigious amounts of work, Dr. Maynard was the creator or catalyst of many significant projects during his forty years of service to Methodist and United Methodist church organizations. He initiated the Spanish program journal only a year after launching the English journal; he then took Spanish classes that he might better serve the Spanish-speaking members. He also worked for five years with Native Americans to help improve their regional and national communications.

A journalist of strong opinion, Maynard was a proponent of simplified spellings that were being urged in many quarters at the time—thus the use of forms like *catalog* and *drouth* in the late '50s.

In 1963 all publications under Maynard's supervision implemented the new ZIP code system, but he refused to let the postmaster dictate that there would be two spaces before the ZIP rather than one.

Years later, provoked by those who repeatedly confused communication with communications, Maynard wrote the definitive memo on the subject (approximately 1,500 words) that is still in use by UMCom editors.

As a high school student in Iowa, Maynard wrote for a weekly newspaper in a small farming town, also learning to set type by hand and to operate the Linotype machine. His career spanned the development of modern high-speed offset printing and computerized writing, editing and typesetting.

After his retirement at the end of 1984, Maynard continued to work for the church as a consultant and free-lance writer. He volunteered as professor of journalism at Shue Yan College in Hong Kong 1986-87 and from 1987 to 1989 was adjunct professor of journalism at United Theological Seminary in Dayton, Ohio.

A Cornell College graduate, Maynard earned the Master of Arts in Journalism degree from Syracuse University and was awarded an honorary Doctor of Humane Letters from Cornell. He also has studied at Northwestern University and with the World Association for Christian Communication in London, England.

Maynard lives in Dayton with Eleanor, his wife of more than forty years. The couple has four grown children and eight grandchildren.